TURN YOUR
Talent INTO
A BUSINESS

A GUIDE TO EARNING A
LIVING FROM YOUR HOBBY

By Emma Jones

brightword

A Brightword book | www.brightwordpublishing.com

HARRIMAN HOUSE LTD
3A Penns Road
Petersfield
Hampshire
GU32 2EW
GREAT BRITAIN

Tel: +44 (0)1730 233870 | Fax: +44 (0)1730 233880
Email: enquiries@harriman-house.com | Website: www.harriman-house.com

ISBN: 978–1–908003–23–2

British Library Cataloguing in Publication Data | A CIP catalogue record for this book can be obtained from the British Library.

Book printed and bound in the UK by CPI Antony Rowe

Set in Caslon and joeHand 2

Contents

Introduction

What better way to earn a living than by doing something you love? That's the position you could be in by following the steps and tips offered in this book.

It has been written in partnership with *Country Living* Magazine after witnessing the success of the Kitchen Table Talent Awards, the most popular competition run by the magazine, and sell-out audiences at the *Country Living* Spring Fair for talks on how to turn a hobby into a business. The team at *Country Living* know their readers have bags of talent; what was becoming increasingly clear is how many of you are considering turning that talent into turnover!

This book will show you how. It presents stories of 17 people who are successfully earning from what started as a hobby or skill and is now delivering decent income. You will discover how to make sales, write a business plan, protect your work, price products and promote yourself.

There's never been a better time to take this onboard and take the first steps to becoming your own boss. You can start whilst keeping hold of the day job, on a bootstrap of a budget and in the knowledge you're not alone; in the 3 months following the launch of the StartUp Britain campaign (a new campaign launched by entrepreneurs for entrepreneurs, designed to celebrate, inspire and accelerate enterprise in the UK) the number of people searching for the term 'start up' increased by 25% and Companies House is recording month-on-month increases in the number of people forming a new business.

People are rapidly realising you can start a business in your spare time and on a budget of less than £100, with the end result being freedom and flexibility to choose where, when and how you work. Indeed one of the great benefits of running a business say many of the case study stories profiled over the following pages, is the ability to shape the business around the family and, in the case of a good number of them, employ family members too!

If being in control of your working life and earning from doing what you enjoy sounds attractive, this is the book for you. Step by step I will show you how to take that hobby, passion or skill and turn it into a business.

I hope you enjoy the journey and that you'll keep in touch along the way.

Emma Jones

emma@enterprisenation.com | @emmaljones

Emma Jones is founder of small business support company Enterprise Nation *www.enterprisenation.com* and a co-founder of StartUp Britain *www.startupbritain.org*.

Enterprise Nation provides daily content, books, eBooks, kits, events and funding to help anyone start and grow a small business.

Foreword

Everyone has a talent for something: a skill, often honed at the kitchen table and used as a way to switch off – from work, family, domestic duties and the increasing amount of admin our lives demand.

Your talent is what you are good at or have a gift for, it's what gives you the most satisfaction, a certain pleasure in knowing you do it well and it is often the basis of a hobby.

But the story doesn't have to end there. There's never been a better time to turn that talent into turnover and this book will help you do that, in plain English and wise words from people who have been there before you.

There's never been a better time to turn your talent into turnover

We at *Country Living* Magazine have been working with Emma Jones and Enterprise Nation through *Country Living*'s Kitchen Table Talent Awards (***kitchentabletalent.com***) to encourage our readers to earn a living from their hobbies. When she suggested that Brightword Publishing would be interested in producing a *Country Living* manual for every life-changing step of the journey from pastime to full-time, we signed up immediately.

By telling their stories in each issue of the magazine, and by promoting them at our *Country Living* Fairs and shows around the country, *Country Living* Magazine has helped hundreds of small businesses launch and grow.

If there's one thing we have learned it is don't be scared by the B word – your 'business' doesn't have to be a *Dragons' Den* contender looking for venture capitalists with big bucks. You might be very local, perhaps only making one item, and your 'factory' could be the spare room but it is perfectly possible to earn an income, especially if you are selling your product to people all over the world through the level playing field of the internet.

Alongside this book you will need passion and persistence but if you sew, make or draw, write, cook or grow then you probably already have these in spades.

So don't be daunted by the stories of success throughout this book, but be inspired. Every one of these businesses started off with a dream and an idea – just like yours!

Lisa Sykes

Features Editor, *Country Living* Magazine

Tell us about your business by posting what you're all about and some pics on Country Living's *Facebook wall at **facebook.com/countrylivinguk** or tweet @countrylivinguk*

Who is this book for?

This book is for anyone who has a passion, skill or hobby and an interest in turning this into a business. You may be baking cakes for friends and family and dreaming of doing this full time or have a way with words that could be turned into commissions. Maybe you paint or draw and wonder if those who offer praise would be prepared to pay for your creations, or whether your flair for fashion could lead to financial return.

Whatever your talent, it's likely you can turn this into a business with customers paying for the quality products or services you offer. Whether artisan or tailor, writer or baker, what you will discover from this book is how to:

* Make sales beyond friends and family

* Promote your brand and become well known

* Register the company and manage the finances

* Embrace technology to save time and money

* Convey a professional image; online and off

* Create a support network and work with partners

Above all, it shows how to make money from doing what you love!

The book is divided into clear chapters with stories throughout of people who have successfully started and grown their own business; from Alex Gooch who is winning awards for his artisan bread, to Jane Fielding who is selling cushioned love letters across the globe, and Kelly and Kev Brett who have built a business around the family and are now expanding into the corporate world. They all offer their stories and top tips for success.

With clear steps, useful links and expert advice, consider this book your guide as you turn talent into a business, and share it with friends and family who are doing the same!

Contributors

With thanks to the following people who have contributed their expertise or story in the compilation of this book ...

Commissioning Editor

Thanks to Louise Hinchen who acted as Commissioning Editor on this book. Without her, this project would not have happened nor this book be in your hands!

Talent into turnover

Emma Henderson, Showpony
Emma Maudsley, Sock Monkey Emporium
Annabel Mills, Annabel Mills
Sarah Thomas, Sarah J. Thomas Photography
Aimee Waller, Château Velvet
Alex Gooch, Alex Gooch Bread
Arianna Cadwallader, Saturday Sewing Session
Alex Johnson, Shedworking.co.uk
Kelly and Bev Brett, Piddley Pix
Kate Shirazi, Cakeadoodledo
Tracey Mathieson, Foxtail Lilly
Ian and Joe Butler, Croglin Designs
Rachel Barker, Rachel Barker
Helen Field, Round Robin Garden Wildlife Supplies

Jo Colwill, Cowslip Workshops
Sue Powell, The Gluten Free Kitchen
Lise Bech, Bech Baskets

Experts

Louise Hinchen, Brightword Publishing
Emily Coltman, FreeAgent
Joanne Dewberry, Charlie Moo's
Louise Findlay-Wilson, PRPro
Cally Robson, She's Ingenious
Mark Shaw, Twitter expert
Greg Simpson, Press For Attention
Jackie Wade, Winning Sales
Laura Rigney, Pitcher House
Mark and Philomena, Business Photography
Niamh Guckian, Totally Wired
Alex Harrington-Griffin, Business Crayon
Mark Glynne-Jones, JumpTo!

Country Living contributors

Lisa Sykes
Ruth Chandler
Hester Lacey
Catherine Butler
Rachael Oakden

Jenny Buist Brown
Caroline Rees
Lee Karen Stowe
Louise Elliott

Chapter One

Making the move from hobby to business

COMING UP WITH AN IDEA

When starting a business, the first step is to come up with an idea for what the business will do and on which of your skills it will be based. Many talented people tell me their problem is not coming up with one idea, it's a case of having too many ideas! In which case, bear in mind that a niche business is often the best kind of business.

Niche is nice

Niche is nice! What I mean by this is: craft your hobby, passion or skill so it becomes a product or service that meets the needs of a very well defined audience. For example, a baker focused on producing speciality goods, such as Alex Gooch profiled on page 182, or handmade luxury cards aimed at customers buying for a special occasion which is Aimee Waller's talent, profiled on page 89.

There are two key benefits to having a niche business:

1. You keep marketing costs low, as your audience is well defined; you know where your audience are and you have researched and understand the kind of marketing messages to which they will respond.

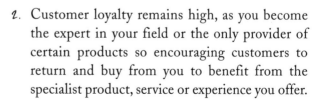

2. Customer loyalty remains high, as you become the expert in your field or the only provider of certain products so encouraging customers to return and buy from you to benefit from the specialist product, service or experience you offer.

Think about how you can fashion your talent into an idea that has a clear purpose for a clearly defined audience.

This book shows how to base a business on what you enjoy making or doing; at the same time, it's important to have an eye on what people will buy. This is reflected in the top tips offered by Emma Henderson (page 101) and Carol Powell (page 23) who say:

> "Get your work out there, tell people it's for sale, tell them how much it costs and make sure it's something people will pay for."
>
> **– Emma Henderson**

> "Research is essential. Make sure that there is a market for your product and research whether potential customers are willing to buy what you enjoy making."
>
> **– Carol Powell**

To solve that issue of having too many ideas, spend time working on them all but focus on the product or service that sells, i.e. let the market dictate the idea that becomes the focus of your attention.

Researching the market

Research your potential customers, the competition and a price point by visiting competitors' sites, online trade sites/forums, reading reports, and seeking intelligence from experts. Look for information that will answer the following questions:

* What is the number of potential customers you can serve, and how do these customers like to be served?
* What are their characteristics, spending patterns and who are their key influencers?
* Who is currently serving your market?
* Where are your potential customers going for their goods and services?

★ What do they like about what they're getting and, more importantly, what do they dislike (as this opens up opportunities for you to improve on the status quo)?

In view of the above, is there a business here? Is there room in the market for your business and is the demand there? If so, you then need to start thinking about what price you could charge for your product/service.

Price yourself at a rate that's competitive with other providers in the market, that takes into account the amount of time, personal service and added value you offer, and that will turn a profit at the end of the day!

Talent into turnover

NAME: KATE SHIRAZI
TALENT: BAKING
BUSINESS: CAKEADOODLEDO

Kate Shirazi, a former health visitor and A&E nurse, initially began her cupcake business by baking batches for friends and family, but her business really took off when she was asked to do the cakes for a friend's 50th birthday party.

"Afterwards I started getting orders in from people who had tried the cakes at the party," Kate says. "I was very lucky as most of my business has come through word of mouth. Although I only tend to cater for large events, such as weddings, in Devon, my gift boxes can be sent all over the country."

The business has expanded to such a rate that every day, Kate's kitchen is lined up with orders. Initially, Kate spent months researching the market and wanted to be able to produce something that tasted as good as it looked. "I bought a cake from a famous London bakery," she says. "For me, it was the pinnacle in design, but when I tasted it I was so disappointed because it was nothing special at all."

As a result of this research, Kate insists on only using the best ingredients, including Green & Black's cocoa and importing her vanilla extract from France, and says that her customers will able to tell the difference if she used anything else.

In the last couple of years, Kate has grown the business and now works from a separate kitchen attached to her house. All Cakeadoodledo cakes are made to order and entirely bespoke, and Kate has now perfected a system of efficient baking and decorating through investing in new commercial mixers and ovens.

This investment also means that Kate can supply local food retailers with pre-packed gift boxes of cakes.

Kate has also had several baking books published, including *Cupcake Magic*, *Cookie Magic*, *Chocolate Magic*, *Baking Magic* and *Cake Magic*. The Cakeadoodledo Kitchen Linen Range launched in January 2010 and is now being stocked by independent retailers nationwide as well as on sites such as Not On The High Street.

Top tip

"Be prepared to work harder than you ever thought possible and if you really believe in something, stick to your guns. If you have doubts, listen to them."

★ *www.cakeadoodledo.co.uk*

Research tools

To find answers to your questions and to source information on competitors, visit forums and sites where your potential customers gather and read up on the local competition. Get on Google, follow links posted on social media sites such as Facebook and Twitter and find out who's out there and what people are saying about them.

Visit competitor websites and consider buying from them, or using their service, to get an idea of their strong points – and maybe their weaknesses too – so that when you come to set up your business, you know what you like and what you don't like!

Another option is to source primary or firsthand data by conducting a survey, posing questions via social media channels or hitting the streets with a clipboard! This can be a great way of getting information direct from your target audience so when you launch the business you know you are positioning it correctly.

Survey tools

* SurveyMonkey | *www.surveymonkey.com*

* Wufoo | *www.wufoo.com*

Social media channels

* Twitter | *www.twitter.com*

* Facebook | *www.facebook.com*

* LinkedIn | *www.linkedin.com*

Carry out research face-to-face by displaying goods at fairs and markets (*see pages 188–190 for advice on how to go about this*) and complete the market research template below to be sure there's a sufficient market of people to buy your products at a price that will turn a profit.

How big is the market?

What is the number of potential customers I can serve and how do these customers like to be served?

. . . .
. . . .
. . . .
. . . .
. . . .

What are their characteristics, spending patterns and who are their key influencers?

. . . .
. . . .
. . . .
. . . .
. . . .

Who is currently serving my market?

Where are my potential customers currently going for their goods and services?

. . . .
. . . .
. . . .
. . . .
. . . .

What do they like about what they're getting, and, more importantly, what do they dislike?

. . . .
. . . .
. . . .
. . . .
. . . .

What price can I charge for my product/service?

What's competitive and takes into account the amount of time, personal service and added value that I offer?

. . . .
. . . .
. . . .
. . . .
. . . .

TIP: What am I worth?

How much do you think customers or clients would pay for your product or service? To begin with, take a look at how similar offerings are priced and talk to your potential customers about how much they'd be willing to pay. Then talk to suppliers to check you can source materials and deliver at a price that covers your costs and still leaves a margin.

Since starting a business from home will save you lots of money, you can pass some of these savings onto your customers, which could give you an edge over other businesses. However, make sure you don't undercharge for the expertise, talent and knowledge you offer.

Also consider charging less for work that will reflect well on your business and boost your reputation, perhaps in the media or with a credible customer.

More information on producing and pricing your products can be found in Chapter Three and Chapter Six, and details on how to create a basic cash flow sheet are on page 94.

Friends and family focus group

When moving from hobby to business, friends and family represent a key focus group and your most ardent supporters. Talk through your ideas and ask for feedback on the product/service itself and your qualities in being able to deliver. Joanne Dewberry rightly says on page 25 that you should test products on strangers too but conversations with friends and family will help you prepare an initial SWOT analysis for the business.

SWOT Analysis

With your idea and research in hand, prepare a SWOT analysis. This stands for: Strengths, Weaknesses, Opportunities, Threats.

Strengths

What are my strengths?

What can I do better than anyone else?

What resources do I have?

What's my unique selling point?

Opportunities

What opportunities do I see?

Does my idea tap into any trends?

Are there any emerging technologies that could help my idea?

Has there been anything in the news related to my idea?

Weaknesses

What are my weaknesses?

What should I avoid?

Where do I lack skills?

What might hinder my success?

Threats

What threats would I face?

Who's my competition?

Does changing technology affect my idea?

Jane Field carried out her market research when she gave Love Letters to her family for Christmas …

Talent into turnover

NAME: JANE FIELD
TALENT: BUSINESS (AND CRAFTING!)
BUSINESS: JONNY'S SISTER

Jane Field's real passion is for business. Combined with a love of fabrics and interiors, she's successfully created Jonny's Sister, a business selling personalised cushions called Love Letters.

"Both my parents had their own businesses and my three brothers work for themselves so I guess you could say it's in the blood. My earliest memory of business is selling jam jars of bees at the bottom of our drive when I was about 5 years old. It came to a sticky end when a potential customer stopped, got out of his car and, upon inspection of my jars, informed me that they were actually wasps!"

Leaving a high-pressure job in London, Jane moved her young family to the country and took a couple of years off to stay home with the children. She then realised that if she started her own business she could work from home and still be on hand for the family.

"The idea of letters literally came to me, as personalisation was just starting to become popular. I designed the template, got the cushions made up by an upholsterer and then gave them to everyone for Christmas. I watched their faces as they opened them to gauge their reaction. Market research at its best!"

A friend then persuaded Jane to send a Love Letter to the Editor of *Country Living* Magazine. This led to the possibility of Jane's cushions being included in the *Country Living* Emporium, which highlights products for the home and garden. Jane had six weeks to finalise the website, source design protection on the products and get packaging designed and produced in time for her products appearing. On the first day of being profiled in the Emporium, Jane received 17 orders.

> "I wasn't sure whether to laugh or cry in panic! Our first customer was a wonderful woman from Wales who bought one for her granddaughter. She is still buying from us today!"

Jane has support in the form of an office manager, a packer and her husband who takes care of company finances. There's also a team of 7 seamstresses who make the products.

> "I'm promoting the business and growing sales through encouraging people to visit the website which is the source of most sales. I do this through Google AdWords, attending fairs, sending out a monthly newsletter, donating products to charity events, running competitions, getting featured in magazines, using social media, selling products through third parties (shops and other ecommerce websites) and telling everyone I meet about our great products!"

Jane and the team work from a large log cabin in the grounds of her house. As well as the benefit of a scenic setting, this has meant Jane has always been around when the children are on holiday and still manages (somehow!) to get in a full day's work.

> "During the school holidays if the weather prevents camping the children will often sleep out in the cabin with friends, especially as we have a huge cutting table that doubles up as a table tennis table!"

Jane plans to continue growing the business over the next 12 months with help from friends and experts. She is a big believer in accepting you can't be great at everything and to concentrate on what you're good at and ask someone who has been there and done it to help in weaker areas.

"Equally as important, though, is that once you're up and running and have some experience under your belt, you should offer to do the same. We are all in this together and the sooner people realise that the sharing of experience is a positive exercise, then the more successful we will all be in business."

Top tip

"Have a USP (unique selling point), stand out from the crowd and dare to be different!"

★ *www.jonnysister.co.uk* | @jonnyssister

The name game

Coming up with an idea and carrying out research will get you thinking about what to name your new baby (by which I mean your business!). If you are selling your knowledge the company may be named after you, for example, 'Emma Jones Advisory Services', in which case, job done. But if that's not appropriate, think of a name that:

★ is easy to spell

★ is not already registered with Companies House (you can use a free webcheck service to access existing company names at *www.companieshouse.gov.uk*) or trademarked

★ people will remember

★ has an available domain name.

You might want to protect the name with a trademark to make sure that no one else can take it in the future. *See page 49 for more information.*

If you get stuck, visit Enterprise Nation (*www.enterprisenation.com*) where you will find people who can help you win the name game, as the site is buzzing with talented copywriters and wordsmiths.

Carol Powell named her company Re-jigged as it rightly describes what she offers; clothes recycled and re-jigged to become new and stylish garments …

Talent into turnover

NAME: CAROL POWELL
TALENT: SEWING
BUSINESS: RE-JIGGED

Carol Powell has always had a talent for sewing and a passion for fashion design.

"I learnt to sew when I was very young and at five years old made dolls clothes engineered from scraps of fabrics and tried to sell them in a local sweet shop! Whilst at school, I took a Saturday job working in a fabric shop and then worked for a local interior designer. Both jobs gave me great experience in cutting fabrics and making clothes. This experience stood me in good stead for Re-jigged."

The beginnings of the company came about when Carol made a dress for her daughter from an old jumper with holes in the sleeves and a shirt Carol couldn't bear to throw out.

When other mums started to comment on the beautiful design, Carol thought she should make some more! In 2009, Carol's talent was turned into a fully-fledged business, creating employment for local mums and helping others with every sale.

> "Before launching, I contacted lots of national charities in order to source unwanted, unusable garments. I wanted clothes that were damaged and of no use to charity shops and eventually decided to support local causes. I also wanted to give something back to those that support me, so in return for clothing donations, for every garment I sell, Re-jigged donates money to charities, schools and groups."

Children from the area are benefiting in other ways as Carol has launched sewing classes to help retain the skills of sewing and embroidery and inspire young people to make the most of their own creative talents.

In a further expansion, Carol is producing kits so customers can create their own Re-jigged clothes. It's a sensible way to scale the business.

> "Making one garment takes a long time and is labour intensive and ideally I'd like more people to benefit from Re-jigged clothing, so we have launched our first kit which is a 'Tank top in a tin' that comes with a needle, thread, wool and instructions on how to make your own garment. These are selling fast and are much quicker to produce than us hand-sewing the garment ourselves.'"

Carol promotes the business through social media and directs people to her professional, well-designed website. She also enters awards such as The Pitch in which she was a 'Best New Business 2010' finalist. Carol encourages people to sign up for her email newsletter so she can keep in regular contact with existing and prospective clients.

The business is run from a granary on the side of Carol's family farmhouse in Herefordshire so this business owner remains on hand to be full-time mum. It's a way of life which has been re-jigged to perfection!

Top tip

"Research is essential. Make sure there is a market for your product and research whether potential customers are willing to buy what you enjoy making."

★ *www.re-jigged.co.uk* | @rejigged

Useful link

★ The Pitch | *www.thepitch2011.com*

See page 181 for details of other awards to enter (including Country Living *Magazine's own Kitchen Table Talent Awards!).*

Top tips for launching your craft business

Joanne Dewberry, founder of Charlie Moo's (*www.charliemoos.co.uk*) and author of *Crafting a Successful Small Business* (*www.brightwordpublishing.com*) provides her top tips to launching your craft business.

1. **Start with something you know** (you can develop other skills behind the scenes). This way you can be confident and know the products are of a suitable quality.

2. **Decide where you will sell,** whether that's on or offline, craft fairs and/or websites.

3. **Research what others are making,** where they sell, the prices they sell at and how they are branded and marketed. Find out if you need any information on your products' packaging. Do they need testing? Do you need any certification? Food or natural products will need ingredients listing, kitchens will need to be inspected by environmental health, toys will need CE testing for health and safety. Make sure you know all of this.

4. **Pricing is vital.** You have to take everything into consideration; factor in waste, shipping, equipment, advertising, utilities such as the internet, electricity, telephones, time and your hourly wage.

5. **Test the market.** Get your products in front of others. Find out what they like, don't like, etc. Talk to family members, bearing in mind they are normally well meaning and may not provide the helpful criticism you need so test on strangers too – a market is a good starting place.

6. **Have fun** – that's why you started in the first place!

The franchise option

Consider buying into a franchise or direct selling opportunity that enables you to develop your hobby/skill whilst being self-employed and benefiting from being part of an entrepreneurial team that provides you with templates, branding, training and help with finances.

Whether your passion is gardening, music, homewares or hospitality, there's a franchise opportunity for you! Five are listed here; you can find 45 more in '50 Fantastic Franchises'. For more information visit *www.brightwordpublishing.com/50fantasticfranchises*

★ Jamie at Home – perfect for anyone with an interest in kitchen and dining accessories, events are held in the homes of friends and their network of friends. | *www.jamieathome.com*

★ Girlie Gardening – green fingers, step forward! Become a Girlie Gardening franchisee and you'll be selling Welly Warmers and gardening gloves to those who spend ample time in the herbaceous borders! | *www.girliegardening.com*

* Neal's Yard Remedies – if selling organic natural health and beauty products is your idea of heaven, this is the opportunity for you to make money and make a difference to customers. | *www.nyrorganic.com*

* Best in Glass – believing that staying in is the new going out, Best in Glass launched to offer entrepreneurial individuals with an appreciation of wine and spirits an opportunity to become consultants and sell products at parties. Perfect for the party lover! | *www.best-in-glass.co.uk*

* Music Bugs – run music and singing classes for children as part of the Music Bugs franchise. Franchisees experience high demand for their award-winning sessions and with exclusive and generous territories up for grabs, there has never been a better time to join their friendly and supportive team. | *www.musicbugs.co.uk*

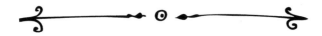

Chapter Two

I'M OFF

BUSINESS PLAN

After coming up with an idea and doing your research, writing a brief business plan is your first practical step to starting your business. With it under your belt you can say, "I'm off!".

A business plan will act as your map; it will guide the business from start to growth, with reference to milestones along the way. For example, you might want to open a shop, launch a website or reach a number of customers within a certain time frame.

The plan will include information about how you intend to get started and what your ultimate objectives are – and how you aim to get from one to the other. You might want to start a business and sell it in a few years' time, or grow to a point where you wouldn't want to grow anymore. And, of course, you'll need to refer to resources: what you have already, what you'll need and how you'll pay for it.

You may also need a plan if you're looking to raise money, from friends or family or from the bank.

With it in hand, you'll be off on your business journey. Or IMOFF.

It's an easy way to remember the headings to include in your business plan: Idea, Market, Operations, Financials and Friends.

Idea

What's your idea?

Market

Who will be your customers or clients? And who is your competition?

Operations

How will you develop the idea, promote it, and provide good customer service?

Financials

Can you earn more than you spend, so that the business makes a profit? Do you need any funds to get started?

Friends

Do you have a support network on hand for when you need business advice? Are there complementary businesses you've identified with whom partnerships are a possibility?

Have these as headings in your plan and you've taken a big step closer to becoming your own boss.

TIP: Revisit regularly

Review your plan regularly to check progress against targets or to make amends as you respond to new opportunities. I revisit the Enterprise Nation plan for a 'gentle' recap every six months and then at the start of each year head off for a couple of days to re-read the plan, rethink the business, and rewrite if required.

BUSINESS PLAN TEMPLATE

Use this template to write your own business plan.

Executive Summary

....
....
....
....
....

The Idea

....
....
....
....
....

The Market

Customers

....
....
....
....
....

Competition

. . . .
. . . .
. . . .
. . . .
. . . .

Operations

. . . .
. . . .
. . . .
. . . .
. . . .

The CEO

. . . .
. . . .
. . . .
. . . .
. . . .

Sourcing

....
....
....
....
....

Sales & Marketing
Press

....
....
....
....
....

Online

....
....
....
....
....

Partners

. . . .
. . . .
. . . .
. . . .
. . . .

Systems

. . . .
. . . .
. . . .
. . . .
. . . .

Friends & Family

. . . .
. . . .
. . . .
. . . .
. . . .

Talent into turnover

NAME: IAN AND JOE BUTLER
TALENT: TOY MAKERS
BUSINESS: CROGLIN DESIGNS

Established in 1980, Croglin Designs have built their business on the multi-generational appeal of handmade wooden toys and have succeeded in producing quality items in a market that is saturated with cheap, mass-produced toys.

The business began when Ian and his wife Ruth moved to Croglin, an isolated Eden Valley farming village, and he turned to his hobby of woodwork to pay the bills. Working in a friend's workshop with a few basic tools and secondhand materials, Ian started slowly and Ruth would sell some of the toys at a local market if there was an available stall, using any money made to support the family. Their son Joe was just two weeks old the first time he accompanied his father to a craft market.

By the time Joe was at university in Plymouth, Croglin Designs had moved six miles across the Eden to Lazonby, but a career in toymaking was the last thing on Joe's mind. However, during a visit home he used his father's workshop to make a chopping board to take back to college, and his love of wood was kindled. "I started to appreciate its character and variety – you never know how it is going to look until it's finished," he says.

In over 30 years the business has barely changed. Both father and son continue to make each toy in their workshop at home with the help of hand-operated machinery, personally cutting and sanding until each product is complete. As Ian recognises, there are few companies who produce toys as they do. "There are very few people still producing toys the way we do, because it is so hard to make it pay," he says, and so part of Joe's role is to look into modernising techniques that will still allow them to produce the craftsmanship they have become renowned for.

"Occasionally we have different opinions about the way forward. But with Joe on board, ours is a young, dynamic business again, instead of growing old like the majority of the toymakers," Ian says.

Top tip

"Seek out feedback from a non-biased source. Sometimes people are too polite and send you on a wild goose chase, so don't listen to every negative but ignore them at your peril! Good designs come from continual tweaking after feedback."

★ *www.croglindesigns.co.uk*

Chapter Three

The must-dos – registering the company and protecting your brand

A s the business comes into being, so does a duty to register the company as a trading entity. There's also the company assets to consider (brand/name/idea) and how to protect them.

REGISTER THE COMPANY

When you set up in business there is one key organisation to contact and inform: HM Revenue & Customs (HMRC). You may also need to register with Companies House. Before contacting either, have a think about the company status that suits you best. There are a number of options:

Self-employed

As it sounds, this means working for yourself; you keep records and accounts of your own activity, and, in acting alone, get to keep all the profits – but are also solely liable for any debts.

If you set up as a self-employed sole trader you don't need to register with Companies House or take on any of the accounting duties that come with being a limited company, as outlined below.

Partnership

If you'd like to be self-employed but want to work with a friend or colleague, consider a partnership. It means that two or more people share the risks, costs, profits and workload. Partnerships do not have to file accounts at Companies House but there are filing requirements with HM Revenue & Customs, as outlined below. A limited liability partnership or LLP is structured in the same way as a normal partnership but, as it sounds, limits the liability of each partner. An LLP has the same filing requirements at Companies House as a limited company.

Find out more about the legal status of partnerships on the Business Link site at: *tinyurl.com/6k7dmml*

Limited company

Limited companies exist in their own right, with the company's finances kept separate from the personal finances of its owner(s). Limited companies have filing responsibilities with both Companies House and HMRC as noted below but it's now much easier to launch a limited company as there is no longer a need to appoint a company secretary, so you can be a limited company with a headcount of one, which many small businesses are!

The status of your company will affect how much admin you have to do and the kind of financial records you must keep and file. Take advice from your accountant or local tax office on which one to choose as much depends on the type of business you will be running.

TIP: Being social

Should you decide to start a social enterprise – a business trading for social and environmental purposes – there are additional legal structures to consider, including:

* community interest company (CIC)

* industrial and provident society

* charitable status.

To find out more about launching a social enterprise or creating a community interest company (CIC) visit:

* Social Enterprise Coalition | *www.socialenterprise.org.uk*
* CIC regulator | *www.cicregulator.gov.uk*

Companies House

When registering with Companies House there are two options from which to choose. You can buy a 'ready-made' company from a company formation agent, or 'incorporate' a company yourself by sending documents and a registration fee to Companies House. If you decide to complete registration yourself, download the form from *bit.ly/ezw1S*.

HM Revenue & Customs

The rules on registering a new business with HM Revenue & Customs are pretty clear-cut. You are required to register as soon as you start earning from any business activity. As above, you can choose to register as self-employed, as a partnership, or as a limited company. Each category has its own filing requirements, as outlined below.

Sole trader/ self-employed

The calculation of tax due and National Insurance owing is done through self-assessment.

You either need to complete form CWF1 or call the newly self-employed business helpline. This should be done within three months of undertaking your first piece of self-employed work in order to avoid a fine.

* Form CWF1 | *www.hmrc.gov.uk/forms/cwf1.pdf*

* Helpline for the newly self-employed | 0845 915 4515

It's not onerous to complete the form and, once registered, you'll be classified as self-employed and sent a self-assessment tax return each year, which you complete, showing your income and expenses from self-employment as well as details of your employment elsewhere (if applicable).

You will be subject to tax and National Insurance on any profits you make, but the good news is that any losses incurred can be offset against your employed income (if you have any), which could even result in a tax rebate.

Depending on your turnover and how straightforward your tax affairs are, you may be able to complete the Short Tax Return (SA200). However, this cannot be self-selected, nor is it on the HMRC website or orderable; HMRC will send it to you automatically if they think you qualify, based on information given in the previous year's return. If you have turnover below £68,000, it's likely that you will qualify. As ever, though, it will depend on individual circumstances, and the law (and various criteria it uses) may change!

Deadlines

Self-assessment tax return deadlines are as follows:

* paper tax returns should be received by HMRC by 31 October of tax year ending 5 April.

* online tax returns should be completed by 31 January (giving you an extra three months).

TIP: Useful links

★ Leaflet SE1 – 'Thinking of working for yourself?' | *www.hmrc.gov.uk/leaflets/se1.pdf*

★ Helping you understand self-assessment and your tax return | *www.hmrc.gov.uk/sa*

Partnership

According to HMRC, a partnership is where:

> "Two or more people set up a business. Each partner is personally responsible for all the business debts, even if the debt was caused by another partner. As partners, each pays income tax on their share of the business profits through self-assessment, as well as National Insurance."

In terms of filing requirements, each partner should complete a partnership supplementary page as part of their individual self-assessment tax return. This is in addition to a partnership return, which has to be submitted by one nominated partner and show each partner's share of profits/losses.

Deadlines

The deadlines for partnership tax returns are as follows:

★ paper tax returns should be received by HMRC by 31 October of tax year ending 5 April

★ online tax returns should be completed by 31 January (giving you an extra three months).

See page 248 for guidance on how to write a partnership agreement.

Limited company

As mentioned, limited company's finances are distinct from the finances of their owner(s). What this means is that the company is liable for its own debts, not the individual owners, as is the case if you are self-employed or in a partnership. In April 2008 it became legal to form and run a limited company with just one person, without the need to involve anyone else (prior to this, by law you also needed a company secretary).

As mentioned earlier, you can form a new limited company by registering with Companies House (*www.companieshouse.gov.uk*) or by using a company creation agent.

As well as registering with Companies House, you also need to let HMRC know you are operating as a limited company. You can do this by completing form CT41G (*bit.ly/de4qi9*).

You will also need to set up and register a PAYE scheme as you are an employee of the company.

* Register PAYE scheme | *www.hmrc.gov.uk/newemployers*

* New employer's helpline | 0845 60 70 143

In terms of filing requirements, you must complete a self-assessment company tax return at the end of the accounting period. The return will show the company's taxable profits and whether any corporation tax is owed, and can be filed online at *www.hmrc.gov.uk/ct*. The return should also be filed with Companies House to comply with the Companies Act 2006. This can be done free of charge, using their online WebFiling: *ewf.companieshouse.gov.uk*

On your returns, you can claim wear-and-tear allowances (capital allowances) on any work-related equipment you buy, and also an element of your expenses for working from home. You can also claim travelling expenses, subsistence and a proportion of your phone calls.

Visit the 'Tax allowances and reliefs if you're self-employed' section on the Business Link website to view the tax allowances, deductions and reliefs you can claim: *tinyurl.com/5sjt2sx*

Deadlines

Company tax returns must be filed within 12 months of the end of your company's corporation tax accounting period. More details on these deadlines can be found at: *www.hmrc.gov.uk/ct/getting-started/deadlines*

TIP: In good order

Keep records of your business dealings – this will make it much easier to complete tax returns when the time comes. Keep hold of:

★ receipts of business-related purchases

★ copies of invoices to customers

★ bank statements (especially if you don't have a separate account for the business; *see page 111 on how to start one*)

★ utility bills (if you are starting the business from home and using part of the house for business); they can be claimed as a business expense and so reduce your tax bill.

For advice from HMRC on good record keeping, visit: *www.hmrc.gov.uk/startingup/keeprecs*

VAT

Whichever tax status you choose, if your business turns over more than £73,000 (2011/12 tax year), or you think your turnover will soon exceed this amount, you should also register for value added tax (VAT).

You can voluntarily register at any time. Being VAT-registered can bring credibility with certain customers, but adding VAT to your invoices may make you more expensive than competitors and you will have to file a VAT return four times a year.

★ How and when to register for VAT | *www.hmrc.gov.uk/vat/start/register*

Accountant accompaniment

Talk to a qualified accountant about the structure that is best for your business. And consider employing their services to complete your tax returns. Even if your accounts are very simple, it is well worth seeking professional advice, particularly as the rules and regulations can change frequently and without warning.

Find an accountant by visiting:

★ ICAEW (Institute of Chartered Accountants in England and Wales) | *www.icaew.com*

★ List of Sage-accredited professionals | *www.sage.co.uk/partner*

★ Accountant partners of online software tool FreeAgentCentral | *www.freeagentcentral.com/partners*

★ Enterprise Nation has an online marketplace of business service providers | *www.enterprisenation.com*

TIP: Useful links

* Starting in Business | *www.hmrc.gov.uk/startingup*

* Tax Help and advice for small business | *www.businesslink.gov.uk/taxhelp*

Business rates

The final form of tax to bear in mind is business rates. If you have applied for planning permission or your local authority is aware you are running a business from home, they may try to charge you business rates as opposed to council tax on the part of the house being used for business purposes, Business rates are different in each area and something that should be discussed with your local authority.

* Business Link on business rates | *bit.ly/grAgTp*

See page 53 to determine if you need to contact your local authority about planning permission and therefore the applicability of business rates.

PROTECT THE BRAND

You have now registered with HM Revenue & Customs and possibly Companies House. Your final consideration should be your intellectual property. You may decide to register a trademark to protect your company name or brand or, if you've come up with a unique invention, a patent. This means that companies can't come along and use your name or invention without your permission.

The four forms of IP

There are four different kinds of intellectual property that you can protect.

1. Patents

These are, essentially, what makes things work. For example, says the Intellectual Property Office (IPO), "what makes a wheel turn or the chemical formula of your favourite fizzy drink".

2. Trademarks

These are "signs (like words and logos) that distinguish goods and services in the marketplace".

3. Designs

What a logo or product looks like, "from the shape of an aeroplane to a fashion item".

4. Copyright

An automatic right that comes into existence for anything written or recorded.

Visit the UK Intellectual Property Office website to carry out searches, register trademarks and read up on all things IP-related.

* Intellectual Property Office | *www.ipo.gov.uk*

We asked Cally Robson from She's Ingenious, The Association for Women with New Product Ideas and Inventions, for her advice about getting your products registered and protected by the Intellectual Property Office:

Q. **Is IP protection as important whether you're delivering products or services? i.e. whether I'm selling a homemade pot or a poem, should I still consider protection?**

A. Yes. Whatever the nature of your business, to distinguish yourself from the competition you need to be unique in some way. IP law basically offers a way to protect what is special about your business. Although IP might feel less relevant in a service-oriented business, it is just as key. Registering a distinct logo and/or name as a trademark, buying a strong web address, and building your brand should all be part of the IP strategy for a service-based business.

Q. **What is the difference between patents, trademarks and copyright?**

A. It is important to understand the differences between forms of IP protection. There are great guides on the Intellectual Property Office website *www.ipo.gov.uk*.

But basically, patents protect concepts that are technically innovative, copyright gives automatic protection to anything that can be put down on a piece of paper, and trademarks protect the name and/or logo of your business. Don't forget design protection too – as well as being able to register designs, it is little known that you also have automatic protection.

Q. **How much will it cost to protect my idea or product?**

A. How long is a piece of string!

Although they look cheap to register, patents can be expensive to maintain, running into hundreds of thousands of pounds if you want to take your concept worldwide. So they tend to suit ideas that have big market potential.

By contrast, registered designs might cost just a few hundred pounds. But they are a weaker form of protection – they can't block someone else from tweaking your design and taking the same basic concept to market.

Registering your own trademark costs just a couple of hundred pounds.

The IPO website has a basic confidentiality agreement you can download for free and amend to suit your specific needs, to protect your ideas in discussions.

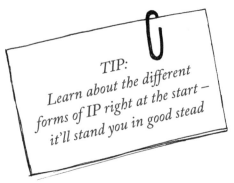

TIP:
Learn about the different forms of IP right at the start – it'll stand you in good stead

Q. **At what stage in the business set-up should I seek protection?**

A. Right at the start you should learn about the different forms of IP and how protection works. The insights you gain could drastically affect how you shape your business and its future ability to be distinctive, block competitors, scale up, and command pricing that will earn you profits.

Q. **Would you recommend taking advice via the IPO website or commissioning an IP expert?**

A. Definitely learn the basics from the IPO website first, and also The British Library's Business and IP Centre in London. Make use of the free first sessions provided by IP experts to ask detailed questions. But always, always before you commission an IP expert, absorb as much as you can from the experience of seasoned entrepreneurs and inventors. Understanding the subtleties of how IP protection actually works in business is essential if you want to grow a sustainable, thriving enterprise.

Useful links

* She's Ingenious | *www.shesingenious.org*

* Intellectual Property Office | *www.ipo.gov.uk*

* British Library IP Centre | *www.bl.uk/bipc*

HOUSEHOLD ADMIN

With a business plan prepared, the regulatory bodies informed and your intellectual property protected, it's time to take care of the household admin and make friends with the neighbours!

Over 60% of businesses are started from home on account of the low costs and lack of commute. When you start and grow your business from home, you may have a few questions about whom you need to inform. Here are the answers.

Q. **Do I need planning permission?**

A. You'll need planning permission to base the business at home if you answer 'yes' to any of these questions:

* will your home no longer be used mainly as a private residence?

* will your business result in a marked rise in traffic or people calling?

* will your business involve any activities that are unusual in a residential area?

* will your business disturb the neighbours at unreasonable hours or create other forms of nuisance such as noise or smells?

If your house is pretty much going to remain a house, with your business quietly accommodated within it, then permission shouldn't be required. If you're unsure, contact your local council to seek their views.

★ *www.planningportal.gov.uk*

Q. **Do I need to tell the local authority I'm working from home?**

A. This depends on whether you pass the planning test. If you need planning permission, you'll have to inform your local authority. If you don't, then the only benefit of telling them is that they'll charge you business rates (rather than council tax) on the part of the house being used for business purposes. Business rates are different in each area and something that should be discussed with your local authority.

★ Business Rates information from Business Link |
www.businesslink.gov.uk/businessrates

Q. **Do I need to tell the landlord?**

A. Yes, it's best to let them know that you will be working from home. The good news is that the coalition government announced on 1 November 2010 that social landlords should review any contracts prohibiting people from running a business from home.

Q. **Do I need to inform my mortgage provider?**

A. Yes, it's best to let them know – even though it shouldn't mean any change in the mortgage repayment.

Q. **What about my insurance provider? Do they need to know?**

A. Yes, do inform your insurance company. Tell them about the equipment and stock you have at home. An upgrade from domestic to a business policy is not usually expensive so don't be put off in making this call. Your insurance provider is likely to recommend that you also take out public liability insurance in case anyone who comes to visit suffers an injury in or around your home office. *See page 93 for details of the type of insurance you may need.*

Q. **Do I need protection for when customers and contacts come to visit?**

A. Yes, carry out a health and safety check, which is easy to do by following the steps set out by the Health and Safety Executive in their homeworking guide (PDF available at *www.hse.gov.uk/pubns/indg226.pdf*).

* Health and Safety Executive | *www.hse.gov.uk*

Q. **Should I tell the neighbours?**

A. Yes. *See the next section for more advice!*

Everyone needs good neighbours

When working from home it's worth keeping your neighbours sweet and firmly on side. You don't want them getting annoyed by any deliveries or unusual distractions.

Explain to your neighbours that you are running a business from home and that it shouldn't cause them any disturbance. (If it will cause them disturbance, see above: you'll need planning permission!)

Keep your promise and try to keep disruptions to a minimum. Avoid big heavy deliveries at anti-social hours and streams of client traffic clogging up the roads.

If the business reaches a major milestone, maybe host a party for your neighbours. A friend of mine said his neighbours were more than happy to 'be on the telly' when his home business appeared on a Sky News live broadcast from his home office!

Make friends with other homeworkers in your neighbourhood, so you can demonstrate together that the way you work is beneficial to the economy of the area and its safety, for example you can keep an eye on your neighbours' houses during the day.

If you know of a time when there'll be an unusual amount of activity in your home office, let your neighbours know in advance and perhaps send a bottle of wine to thank them for their cooperation.

Talent into turnover

NAME: RACHEL BARKER
TALENT: POTTERY
BUSINESS: RACHEL BARKER

Rachel Barker is a small family-run business based in Shropshire that designs and produces gorgeous ceramics. Run by Rachel and her partner Andrew, the business really took off when they moved from Bristol to the countryside.

"The move definitely made a difference, it has been very fruitful," she says. "Although my work isn't what you'd call 'country', our rural surroundings are definitely a great source of inspiration. It's often the small details, things that are fleeting or incidental, that fascinate me. Rivulets of rain on glass, haphazard lines in a clump of bamboo, saw marks in a chunk of wood. These become the pared down, simple images which integrate well to decorate my ceramics. I don't represent the wider landscape in a formal way, but I definitely use elements from it."

Although both Rachel and Andrew went to art college, it was actually fine art rather than ceramics which they studied, and Rachel believes that may have in fact been a great help to the business. "I wasn't taught what I should and shouldn't do, so I was prepared to think more broadly and adapt to possibilities," she says.

All the items in the Rachel Barker collection are planned, designed, and trialed in their workshop as handmade, one-off pieces; then, as Rachel says, "the proof of the pudding… we try them at home in the kitchen. Without this real experience of how each piece works and making alterations accordingly, the process would be very hit and miss. Only when we are happy with the results can we think about producing and selling."

Rachel can't personally produce her entire range so she has looked externally for ways to do this while still keeping the fundamental elements of her products. "I wanted to have our ceramics more widely available and affordable than I could possibly achieve in our little workshop," Rachel says.

"Be critical yourself – don't just rely on other people's opinion!"

As such, she decided to enlist a long-established company in Stoke-on-Trent, the traditional heartland of British pottery, to make her designs in creamware, a high-quality English earthenware. Rachel says that their skills are crucial to the handmade nature of her ceramics, and even though English production is expensive in comparison with using companies in, for example, the Far East, the qualities they can achieve are very special.

"Each piece is slip-cast by hand; a person with a very big pot of liquid clay pours it into our moulds," Rachel explains. "Although it's an industrial process, it's done in the traditional way, and the results are down to the skill of specific individuals using their years of experience to make each item just right."

She also uses two small Midlands firms to print her fabric and make up her textile range, which includes aprons, oven gloves and tea cosies.

Rachel's plans for the future include "extending the range to include more textiles and stationery and there are new ceramics in the pipeline, which is always exciting" she says. "But more than anything, I want to make beautiful ceramics that people will want to use every day."

Top tip

"Use all your critical powers of judgement; don't just reply on other people's assessment or opinion. Only work with capable, trustworthy people – you have to build good working relationships and enjoy working with others to get the best results and there are some sharks out there who you should avoid – you will know them when you meet them!"

★ *www.rachelbarker.com*

TIP: The benefits of a home-based business

There are benefits to the business, and to your life, in starting a business from home:

Work benefits

The 60-second commute!

Getting more done, without distractions

The financial savings

Being able to give your clients personal service and a homely welcome when they visit the office

Adding to the property value of your home (research carried out on my website showed that homes with offices sell for an average £25,000 more than homes without offices)

Life benefits

Feeling happier, healthier and more balanced, and enjoying the benefits this brings to your relationships

Wearing what you like

Dancing in the office!

Being a friend to the environment

Going shopping when there are no queues

Alex Johnson has worked in spaces from Real Madrid's training ground to a cellar in Hertfordshire but you can't beat working from a shed, he says. Alex runs the popular blog Shedworking as well as generating revenue from other forms of writing …

Talent into turnover

NAME: ALEX JOHNSON
TALENT: WRITING
BUSINESS: SHEDWORKING.CO.UK

Alex Johnson's love of the written and spoken word was born at a young age.

"I've always enjoyed playing with words, from dictating annotations to my Miffy books to my mother before I could write, to the present day where I work online far more than in print. My English teachers at school were very encouraging, but it was probably when I sold an article to *History Today* magazine when I was 17 that I first genuinely realised that what I wrote could be entertaining for others. And make me money."

Since leaving university, writing has been at the centre of everything Alex has done even though, he admits, much of what actually earns the money is either playing with other people's words (he's a digital sub for the online version of *The Independent*) or selling advertisements for his highly popular Shedworking blog, rather than actual 'writing'. The work is varied and Alex is living testimony to the fact writing can be turned into a living.

"At the risk of sounding pompous, I've always felt that if you regard yourself as a 'writer' you ought to be able to turn your hand reasonably successfully to any kind of written communication, long or short, commercial or non-commercial – I've enjoyed working at women's weeklies and on blue chip companies' internal newsletters as much as blogging on a daily basis and writing books. The variety of it all helps to keep my work fresh and, I hope, interesting. Of course some pay better than others, but with quite a wide spread of clients, it means I don't have to rely heavily on just one or two good payers."

New work comes Alex's way almost entirely by word of mouth recommendation or from repeat customers. Alex does very little by way of deliberate promotion of his work (though he does tweet about it quite frequently!) but there's 'pleasant synchronicity' in Alex's words – whereby the blog, for example, has been a good advertisement for his interest in working online and brought in work as a webmaster, while speaking at Media Trust events about journalism has led to work from a cricketing charity magazine looking for an editor.

"I've worked in all sorts of spaces in various countries, from Real Madrid's training ground to a suburban Hertfordshire cellar, but nothing has come close to working in a garden office, which is why I set up the Shedworking website. It's a perfect place to work, a creative den of seclusion which offers the ceremony of going to the office but with a 30 second commute. It's the creative element that every shedworker I've met has commented upon, a space where you can really work efficiently (and comfortably)."

One of the main reasons Alex decided to work from home was to be close to his family.

"It's a terrible cliché, but you only get to see your children (I have three smallish ones) grow up once and being at home means that I can be with them through their early years. It also means I can spend more time with my wife, which is nice. And in purely logistical terms, it means that school runs, cubs pickups, etc., are much, much easier to sort out."

Over the next 12 months Alex has plenty to keep him busy including promotion of his new book (*Bookshelf*) published in January 2012, building the Shedworking brand in the

US, publishing a series of eBooks, and doing more online work for one of his charity clients. That's plenty enough words to write for this talented and creative wordsmith!

Top tips

1. "Don't think you have to make millions to be successful – being small and moderately successful and happy is a major achievement.

2. "Make good use of your contacts – I'm now working for somebody who has hired me three times over the last 20 years for big jobs.

3. "Don't do it from the kitchen table, do it from a garden office!"

★ *www.shedworking.co.uk* | @shedworking

Chapter Four

Create the perfect work environment & top tech tips

O ne of the great benefits of being your own boss is the ability to work where and how you like, whilst wearing what you like!

Create an environment to suit you and equip your office with all the technology, tools and accessories that will deliver a productive end result.

SETTING UP WITH IT

Building the right IT system for your business needn't mean starting from scratch or spending lots of money. Once your business grows you can upgrade your technology as and when funds become available. To start with, there are affordable, even free, solutions that can get you up and running in no time at all. Chances are that you have some of them already! So, let's take a look at what you might already have and what you might need to buy. And we'll separate them by hardware and software.

Hardware

Hardware is the physical components of your IT system. At a basic level, it includes things like your keyboard and mouse, but can extend to include new devices and gadgets that we'll look at in a moment. First, let's list the basic components of a start-up IT system.

Computer

When starting out, using your home's shared computer will be just fine. Bear in mind, however, that in the first few months of starting your business you may find yourself working more hours than usual, trying to get it all set up – so prepare cohabiting friends and family for the possibility of reduced access!

Also, when your business grows, the data you accumulate – information on your customers, clients and contacts, including financial details – will become more and more valuable. You might then think twice about sharing your computer with the rest of the family.

For that reason, and the flexibility you'll have in deciding when and where you can work, I'd recommend looking into buying a separate laptop computer if you don't have one already.

There are affordable – even free – tech solutions to get you up and running in no time.

There was a time when doing so was much more expensive than buying a desktop computer, but in recent years the prices have almost levelled off. Budget laptops start at around £300, but when buying computers it's important to buy the best that you can afford. It'll help you prepare for the future, when new software is released with new demands on your hardware; it'll help you run more programs at once and hold more data, as your business grows; and it'll take the sting out of your purchase when prices start to drop in a few months time!

If you've decided to buy a new computer, here are the things to look out for:

Processor

The processor is the speed of your computer. The higher the number, the faster your computer can run.

Memory

More memory (RAM) means faster overall performance and enables your computer to run more programs at once. Try and buy a computer with as much RAM as you can afford. A common frustration amongst computer users is how long it can take to launch programs and switch between them. More RAM equals less waiting.

Hard drive

The hard drive gives you space for all your data and programs. This can easily be expanded with a second, external hard drive, but you'll be surprised at how quickly it will fill up, especially if you're also storing personal data, like music and photos, on your computer.

Display (for desktops)

You'll be hard pressed to find a computer that comes with a big, CRT display nowadays. Most are sold with slim, flat-screen monitors. If you don't have one already, consider upgrading. You'll save lots of space in your office and, if you get a bigger screen with a higher resolution, you could get more work done, as you'll have more virtual workspace to open programs and documents.

Standard features

You should expect to find an optical drive, for 'burning' CDs and DVDs, and wireless connectivity, so you can get on the internet wherever you are, with all new computer purchases.

Peripherals

Peripherals are devices that can be used with your computer but are not an integral part of it. I don't want to call them 'accessories', because some of the peripherals I use, I couldn't live without!

Multifunction printer

Even though I find myself using it less these days, with most information passed around electronically, I still think it's too early to pronounce the printer dead, especially if you use a multifunction printer like I do.

It's a real space-saver – imagine keeping a printer, scanner, photocopier and fax machine in one office! You'd have no room to do any work. Mine sits neatly on my desk and is particularly handy when I want to email sketches to my designer. He uses his to archive printed documents. When he receives important letters, for example, he scans them into his computer and recycles the hard copy! We're both on our way to paperless home offices.

Backing up your data is vital. Imagine losing all your customer and accounts information ...

External hard drive

I've already mentioned external hard drives. They're great for extending the storage capacity of your computer – so you can keep more data and programs – but they're especially useful for backing up the entirety of your machine. This is a vital process which you should do regularly – imagine the implications if your computer crashed and wouldn't reboot; or if something worse happened. Look for ones with USB 2.0 connections or, if you're using a Mac, a relevant FireWire connection.

They're easy to set up – you just plug them in and they show up in your operating system as another drive. You can then just drag and drop important folders or use special software that automates the process for you. Macs have this software built-in, as do the latest PCs. If not, try SuperDuper! for the Mac and True Image for the PC.

* SuperDuper! | *www.shirt-pocket.com/SuperDuper*

* True Image | *www.acronis.com*

Webcam

A webcam enables you to video chat with clients and contacts and is useful when you need to have a 'face-to-face' meeting but can't get away. Most Macs have webcams built into their screen; for PC webcams try Logitech.

* Logitech | *www.logitech.com*

Speakers

Liberated in being your own boss and working in your own office, listen to your favourite music whenever you like! If you're a music fan treat yourself, and your iTunes library, to a good pair of speakers. Some are designed to be a treat for the eyes as well as the ears. Our favourite set is made by a company called JBL.

* JBL Home Audio | *www.jbl.com*

Keyboard and mouse

Years ago, mice used to work with a ball inside that would be pushed around your desk on a mouse pad. But nowadays, there's a new technology – optical – which means no moving parts and no way for dust to get inside and interfere with the sensors. If you don't have one already, you should get one!

Again, Logitech do a nice range. They also have some good keyboards, some of which are ergonomically designed to prevent repetitive strain injury (RSI) and wireless to cut down on clutter. Have a look around for a keyboard and mouse set and save money.

* Logitech | *www.logitech.com*

VoIP phones

You can make serious savings on your phone bill by using a VoIP phone. VoIP stands for voice over internet protocol and it basically means making calls over the internet rather than by using your phone line. As such, it's a much cheaper way of making calls (it's sometimes free). And it's the easiest way to set up a second phone line. The VoIP phone I use is made by a company called IPEVO, who make handsets in black or white to go with your Mac or PC.

* IPEVO | *www.ipevo.com*

Software

Software consists of the programs and operating system that your computer uses. Again, you'll be using many of them already in your everyday life, so there's no need to splash out when setting up your business. Once it grows you can upgrade to more advanced versions if required. Below are the basics and later we'll look at software (much of it free or very affordable) for when your business is up and running. *See pages 233 and 246 for details.*

Office software

By far the industry standard in office software, for both Mac and PC computers, is Microsoft Office, which includes a word processor as well as presentation and spreadsheet program.

★ Microsoft Office for small business | *office.microsoft.com/en-gb/small-business*

If you're trying to bootstrap try free alternative OpenOffice. It does pretty much everything that Microsoft Office can do, plus it can open and save Microsoft Office files too. It does take some getting used to, but the support is pretty good. It's worth a try!

★ OpenOffice.org | *www.openoffice.org*

TIP: Getting connected

You'll need broadband right from the start: during your research, while you're setting up your business, through to when it grows and takes over the world!

Tablets and smartphones also boast powerful office software for work on the go

Your two main options are ADSL broadband, which is offered by companies like BT and Sky, and cable broadband from Virgin Media. The biggest difference is that ADSL requires a phone line, while cable broadband does not.

The advantage of cable broadband is that if you don't have a landline phone, and always use your mobile, you can save money by not having to pay line rental on your phone as well as on your internet connection. It's often faster, too, but you'll need to check whether it's available in your area. ADSL broadband is more commonplace and there are lots of companies offering it.

As always, read the fine print before you sign anything. Here are some things to look out for:

Price

Some broadband prices seem really cheap but often the prices advertised are for the first few months of an 18-month contract, so make sure you know what you're getting into before you sign anything.

Usage

Some broadband companies will set restrictions on the amount of data you can download in a month and sometimes even charge you extra if you go over your agreed limit. These limits rarely affect most users, but if your business is the kind that needs to send and receive lots of information, look for deals with generous monthly download allowances. Or, better still, unlimited downloads.

Customer support

If you're installing broadband for the first time, you might need some help setting up and also, once you're up and running, knowing what to do when your connection suddenly drops. For these sorts of queries it's handy to have good customer support, so check to see what's on offer and, crucially, how much it would cost to call for help.

Network

Setting up a network used to be the work of professionals and, I suppose, in big companies it still is. But setting one up for your home by yourself is much easier these days. Your internet service provider may have already provided you with a router – a device that allows you to share your internet connection with other computers in your home. And many are now giving out wireless routers for free, so you can connect to the internet all around the house – and even in the garden!

There are two types of wireless router: one for ADSL and another for cable internet. Check with your internet service provider to find out which is the best router for your type of connection.

I didn't get a free wireless router with my provider, but a friend recommended one that I can to you too. It's from a company called Netgear, and it looks quite nice too!

* Netgear | *www.netgear.co.uk*

Web browser

All computers come with web browsers pre-installed. It's the program that allows you to see web pages on the internet. PCs typically use a browser called Internet Explorer, and Macs a program called Safari.

Both do a good job, but there's a browser I use that's just as good. It's called Chrome and it's made by the people at Google. It's fast, secure and customisable, so you can add features that will help you do your work and manage your lifestyle. These include features like URL shortening, comparison shopping and changing the way your browser looks. It's a free, small download that won't take up much storage and it works on Macs and PCs.

★ Google Chrome | *www.google.com/chrome*

Email

Again, computers come with email software preinstalled. On PCs the software is called Outlook Express (or on newer PCs Windows Mail) and on Macs it's just called Mail. If you've got Microsoft Office you might use Outlook (or Entourage, as it's called in the Mac version), which is Outlook Express's big sister. It includes calendar and address book features.

@

POP mail vs. web mail

There are two kinds of email – POP and IMAP. Non-web-based email that you usually use in a program like Outlook or Apple's Mail is called POP mail and it works by downloading messages from a server onto your computer. IMAP is becoming more popular, as it is more convenient for those who use email on several devices, like a laptop, a home computer or a smartphone. You can get POP on those things too, but you end up with copies of messages, which can be confusing. IMAP does a better job of keeping everything in sync, so your inbox looks the same, wherever you are.

Web mail is accessed through a web browser, like Google Chrome or Internet Explorer. However, whilst that's very handy and such web mail is widely provided for free through services like Microsoft's Hotmail or Google's Gmail, it is perhaps less professional-sounding than POP mail.

POP mail can be addressed at your domain (for example *emma@enterprisenation.com*). My Hotmail address, on the other hand, is *enterprisenation@hotmail.co.uk*, which doesn't look quite as good!

But there is a solution that Google provides. It's called Google Apps and it allows you to use all of its web-based features, like email, calendar and instant messaging at your own address. It's especially good for small businesses and organisations – and it's free! You just need to own your own domain, like I do: *www.enterprisenation.com*

★ Google Apps | *www.google.com/a*

Instant messaging and VoIP

A great way to stay in touch with friends and colleagues is by instant messaging (IM), which allows you to exchange typed messages over the internet in real-time. So it's not like email, where there's typically a delay in the response. Instant messaging is more like chatting. And if you work from home, it instils an office-like atmosphere in your very own home office.

Lots of instant messaging programs also allow you to make video and voice calls. The program I use is Skype and it integrates text, voice and video chat. It allows me to make free calls to other Skype users and to landline or mobile phones for a small fee, which is deducted from pay-as-you-go style 'Skype credit'.

You can even assign a landline-sounding phone number to your Skype account, so you can receive calls at your computer, using a VoIP handset (*see page 70*), or divert calls to your mobile when you're out and about. It's worth trying it out before you spend money installing a second line.

★ Skype | *www.skype.com*

TIP: Superfast broadband

BT is investing over £2 billion to deliver superfast fibre broadband to two-thirds of UK homes by the end of 2015. If you live in an area with an activated exchange, new speeds will power your business and enable you to work faster online and download rich digital media in no time. Find out if fibre is coming to your home by visiting *www.bt.com/superfastbroadband*.

Support

If you're in need of assistance with anything from hardware set-up to software installation, then call in the help of a local IT expert. You may know a neighbour who's a dab hand at technology. If not, check out one of a growing number of companies who send a 'geek' direct to your door, or visit our site to gain access to a whole range of friendly technical experts.

* Geeks-on-Wheels | *www.geeks-on-wheels.com*

* The TechGuys | *www.thetechguys.com*

* Geek Squad | *www.geeksquad.co.uk*

* Tech Tuesday on Enterprise Nation | *www.enterprisenation.com*

* HP Business Answers group on LinkedIn | *www.linkedin.com/groups/HP-Business-Answers-3692681*

* *50 Top Tech Tools and Tips*, by David Sandy | *www.brightwordpublishing.com*

CREATING THE PERFECT WORK ENVIRONMENT

Create the perfect work environment for you and your business and follow this checklist to ensure you're working profitably and productively.

Find dedicated space

As your business is likely to be based at home, try to create an area in the house that functions as your dedicated workspace. That way you can mentally adjust yourself to be in business mode when in that space. It helps you to know when you should be working and when you should be taking a break.

It will also help make it clear to friends and family that when you're in your home office or studio, you're working. And when the door's closed, it means, 'I'm busy. Please don't disturb'.

This dedicated space could be a spare room, in the attic, under the stairs or even the garden shed. For garden office dwellers, one blog you will like is Shedworking (*www.shedworking.co.uk*). Check out Alex's story on page 60 for more information on how the Shedworking site came about.

A light touch

Lots of light is good for your mood and work pace but avoid too much task-light shining on the computer monitor. As for colours on the walls, go for light shades as they will make the space look bigger, and consider mirrors to bounce light around.

Invest in a good desk and chair

Depending on the nature of your business, you could be spending a good few hours each day at the desk and in your chair, so be sure they're both sturdy and comfortable! Buy a chair that's designed for computer use – and try it out first. Sitting in an awkward position can put your body under stress, so make sure you can adjust the chair's height and angle to suit you. Ideally, your feet should be flat on the floor and your back straight. Getting this right will make working from home so much more comfortable!

Get a good, sturdy desk that can accommodate your computer, monitor, keyboard and mouse. The top of your monitor should be at eye level and the monitor itself about an arm's length away from you.

Double-up

Invest in storage boxes and turn your wardrobes into filing cabinets! Or buy big boxes, label them well and then find a place to hide them away; maybe doubling up as a chair for visitors.

A spring clean

Wondering what to do with all the stuff in the room that you want to use as your home office? Take space with a company like Access Storage and have your goods accessible but out of the way, or give them up to a recycling company such as Green Works or Freecycle, so your unwanted items can go to a home that does want them!

* Access Self Storage | *www.accessstorage.com*

* Green Works | *www.green-works.co.uk*

* Freecycle | *www.freecycle.org*

Vision board

Set goals and stay on track with the use of a vision board.

A vision board is a visual reminder of what you're trying to achieve in your business and personal life and, attached to the home office wall, can act as a useful daily prompt and pep talk!

Buy a basic board and stick to it pictures that represent your ambitions; places you want to visit, targets for the company, and people with whom you enjoy spending time. Glance at it each day to remind yourself of everything you're working for and towards and to measure how the business is doing. Such a board will encourage you to stay motivated and hit the targets you've set as well as maintaining the bigger picture of where you want the business to go.

In Chapter Ten we look at ways to grow the business without outgrowing the home so you can successfully increase turnover whilst still benefiting from the upsides of working from home; that's not a bad vision to have!

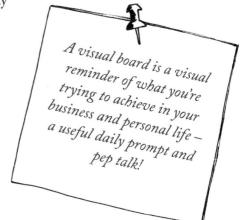

A visual board is a visual reminder of what you're trying to achieve in your business and personal life – a useful daily prompt and pep talk!

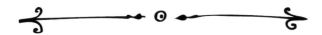

Chapter
Five

*Starting on a
budget and
basic financial
planning*

STARTING ON A BUDGET

Y ou probably already have much of what you need to get started – i.e. a computer, mobile phone, some craft tools – so you might not need to buy much more equipment depending on your business. Here are some tips for keeping initial costs low.

Start the business from home

Why take on the cost of an office when your spare room/attic/garden shed will do just as well? Think of the money you'll save: no premises, no commute, no overpriced sandwiches at lunchtime...! We've already talked about the admin side of starting from home along with information on how to turn a home office into the perfect working environment. Plus if you have children, you can work the business around them so that you get the most out of your time together – not to mention the savings on childcare!

> *Why take on the cost of an office when your spare room/attic/garden shed will do just as well?*

This is what Kelly and Kev Brett decided to do when they started Piddley Pix as a business based from home and around the family ...

Talent into turnover

NAME: KELLY AND KEV BRETT
TALENT: DRAWING
BUSINESS: PIDDLEY PIX

After the birth of their son, Kelly and Kev Brett applied their talent for drawing to produce pictures for the nursery wall. When visitors continued to ask where they had bought such great pieces, this entrepreneurial couple started to think they had the basis for a business. They were right!

"We started to draw more and sold at first to friends and family," says Kelly, "then at a fair and then we produced an album which I would take to work so we started selling to colleagues too! The business just grew from there and almost before our eyes."

With two children now in the Brett family, Kelly continues to work full time whilst husband Kev has decided to stay home to take care of the children and concentrate on drawing. Each Piddley Pix picture is hand drawn and then digitally painted, using a Wacom graphics tablet and pen, with most of the prints being limited editions.

"We make for a good partnership and decided early on that with Kev being the more talented artist, he should stay home to create the product and then my skills kick in as I take care of the admin, promotion, marketing and sales. The strategy and ideas for growing the business come from us working together."

This is paying off. The company is growing with a new line in corporate illustration proving highly popular and introducing Kelly and Kev to a new customer base.

The ultimate plan is for Kelly to be able to give up her day job and join Kev to work on the business full time. Doing so would mean this happy couple spending a lot of time together! How do they manage being life and business partners?

"We both love talking about the business so it's sometimes difficult to stop talking shop but we also appreciate we are parents and husband/wife and as we started this business for the sake of the family, we're very careful to ensure we continue to enjoy family life, outside of the business. So far, so good!"

Top tip

"Be true to yourself and aim to achieve your personal and life goals through the business whilst enjoying time outside the business."

★ *www.piddleypix.com* | @piddleypix

Embrace social media

Make the most of free or low-cost technology tools to raise your profile and make sales. Twitter, Facebook and LinkedIn are excellent places to shout about your work, display photographs and interact with customers and other crafters. Page 209 onwards offers details of the major social media tools and how they can best be used to your benefit.

Beg, borrow and barter!

When starting out, access all the resources you can. On page 182 Alex Gooch tells the story of how he benefited from a generous former employer who allowed him the essential use of a kitchen when he was starting out.

Work 5 to 9

You can plan the business, register the business and indeed continue to run the business successfully by 'working 5 to 9' – this is the term I apply to the five-million-plus people who are holding down a day job and building a business at night and weekends. While you might work as an estate agent during the day, you could get your pottery business up and running in your spare time, giving you the financial security of your full-time job and allowing you to build the business at your own pace.

Working 5 to 9 is a very sensible way to start and grow – you give yourself the time to build confidence and cash flow in the business, plus you can keep putting money aside until you're ready to go full time. See the opposite page for guidance on how and what to tell the boss to make working 5 to 9 as smooth as possible and read Aimee Waller's story to see how she's building her luxury card-making business whilst remaining gainfully employed, with her boss being one of her most loyal customers!

If you're keeping hold of the day job and growing the business in your spare time, here's what you need to do regarding your current job and boss.

The contract

If you have written terms and conditions of employment they are likely to contain reference to the pursuit of personal business ventures outside your contracted working hours. The clauses to look out for include 'the employee's duties and obligations' and what is commonly known as 'whole time and effort'. These clauses usually require the employee to devote the whole of their time, attention and abilities to the business of the employer.

If your contract contains these or similar clauses, don't despair, as it doesn't necessarily mean you can't pursue your business. Many employment contracts are drafted using standard templates with little consideration to personal circumstance. You know your job better than anyone, so if you don't think your business venture will affect the way you do your job, it probably won't – and your employer will recognise this. Having checked how things stand in the contract, it's time to talk things through with your boss.

The conversation

Treat it as an amicable and informal conversation to gauge your employer's initial reaction.

I asked Patrick Lockton, a qualified lawyer and head of Matrix Law Group (*www.matrixlawgroup.com*), for his take on the matter and advice on how employees should go about having this conversation:

"Working 5 to 9 will make you a better, more confident and experienced employee."

"When you approach your employer, be prepared to negotiate, be flexible and compromise. If you think it appropriate, make it clear your business venture will in no shape or form affect your ability to do your job or affect your employer's interests. If anything, it will make you a better, more confident and experienced employee and it will not cost your employer a thing."

Patrick goes on to say:

> "After having such a conversation, you can do one of two things:

> "1. if your employer has not expressed any concerns about your intentions and you have no concerns of your own, disclose your intentions to your employer anyway. Treat it as something you want to do for the sake of clarity and for the record, as opposed to something you want their permission for; or

> "2. if your employer has expressed concerns, try and negotiate a package that you are both happy with. Address their concerns, agree some ground rules and get their permission in writing. Give your employer as much helpful information as possible. If you are going to need some time off or to change your hours then this is the time to bring it up.

> "Always take written notes so that you don't forget what was said and so you can remind your employer what was agreed."

So long as you're not competing with your employer or breaching their trust, you shouldn't have any problem at all in pursuing your 5 to 9 ambitions. After all, as Patrick says, your employer benefits from all the new skills you're picking up, and it doesn't cost them a penny in training or resources!

Aimee Waller is a 5 to 9'er, building her business, Château Velvet, alongside a day job at The Supper Club. Here's how she manages.

Talent into turnover

NAME: AIMEE WALLER
TALENT: CARD MAKING
BUSINESS: CHÂTEAU VELVET

Aimee Waller's parents have been a key influence in where this young business owner is at today. It was her dad who encouraged her to treat life as an adventure and it was from mum that she derived her crafting talent.

> "Mum makes her own clothes and used to make salt dough figures for friends as gifts as well as Christmas tree decorations. I grew up surrounded by this influence so have always liked to make things and have something to show. I think it's the taking of certain ingredients/fabrics/materials and then creating something from it that's special – it's a form of magic!"

Having been brought up to send thank you and birthday cards, Aimee would make her own cards but never quite realised this talent could be turned into a business until she attended a course and met people who gave her the confidence required.

> "I moved to Winchester where I didn't know anyone and had time on my hands. I joined Sue and Sue's workshop and it was the best thing to happen to me (*www.sueandsue.com/workshops.html*).

> "By joining the Christmas decoration workshop I met a whole selection of ladies who admired my work and gave me the confidence to believe in my talent and sell the things I made. I continued to attend their workshops and haven't stopped crafting since!"

Aimee is busy building a business alongside her day job. She gathers materials as and where she finds them; from charity shops, thrift stores, tube seats and department store catalogues. Then it's home to make cards with inspiration from lovely things that surround this budding business owner.

"I try to keep my day job separate from the business but naturally there are times when it does overlap – sometimes you have an idea for a design and you just have to scribble it down, or when you're at an event, 'cards' come up in conversation and you can't help but share your ideas/products with people. My cards are bought by my boss so he is aware of my entrepreneurial spirit and is my most loyal customer. I am very fortunate to be working for The Supper Club, which is a group of the country's most successful entrepreneurs and clearly has its advantages; everything I learn about business I am learning from the best – I just need to start applying it! I work on my cards in the evenings after work and during weekends. I find it very therapeutic and it calms me so doesn't seem like a chore."

Aimee is promoting the business through a blog and via Twitter but most of the promotion comes from word of mouth via existing customers. The first sales came in when Aimee took space at a craft fair which offered an opportunity to sell as well as receive face-to-face feedback from customers.

"I also attended a StartUp Saturday class which was a great chance to meet other aspiring entrepreneurs and focus on the important things to get the business going."

Aimee is now working on a selection of Christmas cards to be sold at craft fairs and hosting a workshop to help others make decorations using recycled papers and magazines.

"Over the next 12 months I hope to have built a website which will enable me to sell my cards online. I'm looking to sell my idea of personalised cards into small boutique shops in areas such as Chelsea and Hampstead. One day I would love for Château Velvet to be a branded shop offering a chance for local people to sell their homemade crafts and to be creative in an environment that encourages creativity and passion."

As this young lady continues on her adventure, we have a good feeling that one of these days that vision will become very real!

Top tip

"Keep doing what you love and what you're good at. I didn't start making cards to sell but to give to my friends with love and I still do that – this just gives me a little extra pocket money! Who says you can't get paid for doing what you love!"

★ *chateauvelvet.blogspot.com* | @chateauvelvet | @aimeewaller

Useful links

★ Sue and Sue | *www.sueandsue.com/workshops.html*

★ StartUp Saturday | *www.enterprisenation.com/events/startup-saturday*

★ The Supper Club | *www.supper-club.net*

TIP: The beauty of barter

Many start-up businesses barter their goods and services, e.g. "I'll produce a sales brochure for you, in exchange for a handmade cushion for my living room." This works well – both parties get what they want. But take heed of the tax implications. Bartering means money doesn't show up in your accounts, but there has been an exchange of goods and services, which implies a taxable activity. The taxman could view bartering as a way to avoid tax. Nevertheless, with so many beneficial arrangements underway, maybe it's time they revised the tax situation?

MANAGING YOUR MONEY

Straightforward finance and easy budgeting techniques

It's become so much easier to start a business on a budget and keep finances in check by keeping overheads low. This section shows how to manage your funds, as well as offering a simple way to calculate profit through use of a basic spreadsheet.

Straightforward finance

When planning a business you'll want to be sure earnings are higher than outgoings.

Earnings are also referred to as revenue, turnover or income and this should be a greater figure than outgoings, overheads or costs. Let's look at the items that come within each category.

Incoming

Earn from selling your product or service and any associated income opportunities. For example, you set up a business selling unique handmade cushions. From the outset, earn income from:

* **Selling** 24 x handmade cushions at £25 per cushion = £600 income per week

* **Speaking** at events to teach others how to make cushions = £150 per event

* **Custom requests**, e.g. a unique and one-off production = £75 per item

* **Developing** a blog on the topic of cushions that attracts cushion-istas as readers and paying advertisers as your secondary customers – £priceless!

Outgoings

Here are the costs; some payable at start-up stage and others ongoing:

* **Salary** – how much do you need to pay yourself? (You will be pleasantly surprised at how thriftily you can live when not commuting.)

* **Property** – start the business from home and avoid the cost of a pricey second office.

* **Raw materials and equipment** – what are the materials you need to deliver and promote your finished cushions? And do you need any equipment to make that product; a sewing machine, computer, printer, smartphone or camera?

* **Insurance** – be insured from the start and choose a policy that covers all your needs.

* **Website/promotion materials** – we will cover on page 153 onwards how you can build a home on the web and promote the business on a shoestring of a budget.

Be insured

There are different categories of insurance which you need to know about to secure the policy that's right for you. The main ones are:

* **Professional indemnity** – relevant to businesses offering services and knowledge and provides protection if you receive a claim alleging a negligent act, error or omission committed by you in the course of the conduct of your professional business.

* **Public liability** – advisable to have if clients are visiting your home office and/or you are supplying goods to consumers. This will protect you in the event of potential injury to business visitors and/or damages arising from the supply or sale of goods which have caused injury to a third party or their property.

* **Business interruption** – covers your potential loss of revenue following a material damage loss.

* **Employer's liability** – only applies when you have employees and offers protection in the event of death or injury to them sustained in the course of their employment.

* **Motor insurance** – This is different to standard car insurance, which does not include business use. If you have a vehicle dedicated for business use to carry stock and/or products, you should buy motor insurance or get a business extension on your car insurance policy when using your existing car for business travel.

* **Home insurance** – You are likely to already have a home insurance policy but this will generally not cover business activities carried out at home or business equipment within the home. Speak to your insurance provider and upgrade to a business policy. This is not usually costly but it will ensure you're protected.

Managing cash flow

Managing cash flow is crucial for the survival of the business, so in order to stay on top of this, keep records of all incomings and outgoings in a basic spreadsheet.

Here is an example spreadsheet you can use:

Date	Client	Work	Amount (exclusive or inclusive of VAT)	Invoice no.	Date invoice sent	Date settled

Keeping records up to date and being on top of invoices means you'll have positive cash flow and so be in a position to buy the stock and supplies needed to make the business function.

The most common reasons for a disruption to cash flow are customers that don't pay, not selling enough products or having too many outgoings, so what can you do to avoid this?

TIP: How to stay on top of your cash flow

* Try to do your cash flow budget regularly so that you always have a clear idea about where your business stands.

* Save costs where possible – you will need to spend some money to get the business up and running but try to keep these to a minimum so outgoings don't start to rack up. *See page 92 onwards for tips on how to achieve this.*

* Have customers pay before you ship their items.

* Plan effectively – if you know there is a craft fair coming up that you want to attend but it might eat into your budget, start planning for this a couple of months early so when the time comes, it isn't a big outgoing expense.

See page 95 for a template invoice and how to keep a record of invoices raised and amounts paid.

Pricing products

When pricing items you don't want to be pricing too high and putting off customers nor do you want to price too low so you don't make any money!

There isn't one simple solution for pricing your products and many crafters will approach this differently, but what's key is to account for the time you take to produce each item; factor this in and price competitively against what others are charging in the market.

Let's take the example of making a handbag and look at how you would work up a price:

The cost for materials including fabric, thread, company labels, zips/buttons and embellishments comes to £3. When deciding how much your materials cost, you don't need to take into account the total price of the supply if you only used a fraction of it. For example, you were able to buy the fabric for the handbags at £2 per metre, but you've only used 1/2 a metre per bag. The estimated cost for the fabric per handbag should therefore be £1.

You then need to add the cost of your time – say it takes one hour for you to make each handbag and you think that your hourly rate is roughly £7.

Now that you have the base cost for your product (£3 for all the materials plus £7 for labour making £10 in total), you need to decide how much you want to mark it up in order to sell to customers.

Many crafters use the 2.5 formula, whereby you multiply base cost by 2.5 and use that as your price. In our example this would make the handbag £25. Once you have that figure, you need to look at your competitors in more detail – are they offering anything similar, and are their products of a similar quality, size, style etc.? Depending on the results of this research, you may want to revise your price, either increasing it if you think your product is worth more, or decreasing it to make it more competitive.

Over time, you may decide you have developed your skill and are producing superior items or sourcing more unique materials so would like to increase prices. Don't be afraid to do this as people will recognise they are buying a unique handmade product and be willing to pay a little extra.

See page 237 for how you might like to grow the business by 'product-ising' your talent – differentiating products by the time it takes to make them.

Talent into turnover

NAME: ANNABEL MILLS
TALENT: CURTAIN MAKING
BUSINESS: ANNABEL MILLS

It was a question of needs must that set Annabel Mills on the path of turning her skill into a business.

> "I needed curtains in our rented house and it was much more fulfilling and cost-effective if I made them myself."

Annabel possessed a passion for fabrics but it was when her children were born that she took up an offer from her aunt who ran a soft furnishings business to have a few lessons in curtain making so this new mum could make good, thick curtains for their rooms.

> "We live in Northumberland, so the focus was on warm, interlined curtains with hand sewn and interesting headings."

These curtains were greatly admired by friends, family and visiting guests and Annabel's first client came in the form of a friend who had just renovated her house and asked Annabel to make the curtains.

> "I didn't charge her much as she was my first client but the deal was that if she liked what I had done she would pass my name onto her friends."

Since then the business has grown solely through word of mouth referrals and in the first couple of years Annabel worked almost entirely for friends or friends of friends taking on one job at a time. The business now attracts custom from people Annabel doesn't know who have been personally recommended and she is taking on bigger jobs and more of them now that the children are at school.

> "I do all the home visits, measuring and curtain-making myself although I now subcontract some of my additional work like cushion covers, window seats and upholstered headboards. I also have a freelance 'curtain fitter' who comes with me to fit poles, tracks and upholstered pelmets – he has made a tremendous difference and means that I now offer a complete service."

Annabel has a workroom at home in a converted garage which gives the space required for a work table (a ping-pong table with a piece of MDF on top of it!), sewing machine and the stocks of lining and interlining. With an upcoming move, Annabel is making sure her network of friends and previous clients know where she's heading so the business can continue to grow. This talented artisan may be moving but the business is coming too!

Top tip

> "Make a start, however small, to test the water and see if there's a market for your product. Put a business card up in your local post office or pub and start spreading the word."

Sourcing supplies and equipment

As with most aspects of the business, research is key! Search for cost-effective and reliable suppliers via the internet or by asking around for personal recommendations.

For example, if you want to run a cupcake business, you could search online for cake supplies and find companies such as:

* Cakes, Cookies & Crafts Shop | *www.cakescookiesandcraftsshop.co.uk*

* Cake Craft World | *www.cakecraftworld.co.uk*

* Cake Craft Shop | *www.cakecraftshop.co.uk*

Or if you want to make wedding invitations, you can find stationery suppliers, such as:

* The Handcraft Card Company | *www.thehandcraftedcardcompany.co.uk*

* Kooky Kards | *www.kookykards.com*

* Papercrafter | *www.papercrafter.co.uk*

These are just a selection of what can be found doing a quick online search.

Online sales sites can also be a great place to source materials. Check out the following websites:

* Etsy | *www.etsy.com*

* eBay | *www.eBay.co.uk*

* Alibaba.com | *www.alibaba.co.uk*

When looking at sourcing supplies, think about how much you're going to use. Even though it's generally more cost-effective, you don't want to interrupt cash flow by buying too much in terms of material and then not receiving the money in from sales, especially if your product has a longer lead time. If buying in smaller quantities, be confident you can get extra supplies quickly if necessary so customers aren't kept waiting!

When it comes to sourcing equipment, if you can't afford to buy new machinery or tools, don't rule out buying second-hand – auction sites and recycling website are useful places to look. Talk to other artisans and crafters as they may be up for sharing tools or upgrading to new equipment and looking for an opportunity to pass on their tools, meaning you get sound equipment at a reduced price.

Emma Henderson was able to reduce prices on a number of her products on account of sourcing a new supplier who could offer preferential rates …

Talent into turnover
NAME: EMMA HENDERSON
TALENT: SCREEN PRINT DESIGN
BUSINESS: SHOWPONY

Emma Henderson's talent has taken her from her spare room to a self-contained studio in the East End of Glasgow. This young screen print designer imports Fairtrade bags from India, applies her unique designs, and sells the finished product to customers across the globe by having a presence on platform sites Etsy and Notonthehighstreet, as well as her own website.

> "Five years in and it still feels like I'm messing about and that one day I'm going to get caught for doing the thing I love and getting paid for it."

Emma promotes the business and her range through attending fairs in London, New York and her home town of Glasgow. Her passion is making products and she's learned along the way the business essentials to get that product to market.

Peer mentoring has helped Emma be sure she's on the right path with her business

> "I picked up what I needed to know about export documentation from the UPS delivery man and when it came to negotiating a deal with a major US store, I asked around, relied on my own wits, and did the deal. Starting and growing a business may appear scary from the outside but when you're in the throes of it, you realise just how much you can achieve."

At times when specific help is required, on business or technical tasks, Emma turns to a fellow artisan. This peer mentoring helps Emma realise she's on the right path with the growth and direction of her own business.

> "I'm planning to grow the business and would consider taking on finance to help do that. Ideally, I'd like to meet someone who has finance and business skills to contribute to the company but until that happens I'll continue to grow organically, making sales online, via wholesalers, and to customers across the globe. It's a great way to make a living!"

Top tip

1. "You just have to go for it. Get your work out there, tell people it's for sale, tell them how much it costs and make sure it's something people will pay for.

2. "In coming up with a price point for my products I compare with what others in the market are charging and then work back to be sure I can make it for that price and still make a profit."

★ *www.showpony.co.uk* | @showpony_design

Top ten finance tips for craft and handmade businesses

Emily Coltman ACA, Chief Accountant to super-straightforward online accounting system FreeAgent and author of *Finance for Small Business* offers her top ten financial tips for small craft businesses.

As a craft business you'll almost certainly be buying and selling stock. This might be raw materials; for example, if you're making curtains, then your raw materials would be the lining fabric, curtain fabric, thread and trimmings. Or you might buy in stock to sell on as is, for example if you're importing silk kaftans from Thailand to sell.

1. Choose your accounting system wisely

It's important for any business to keep their books in order from Day 1, but for owners of craft businesses this is even more important than usual, as you'll be dealing with stock and you'll need to keep track of how much you have at any one time.

Choose a good accounting system with the right level of stock control for your business.

If you're buying in stock to sell straight on, you'll need a system with light stock control. In which case, try FreeAgent *www.freeagentcentral.com*.

If you're making products from raw materials, particularly if your business is growing, look for a system with in-depth stock control. I like Brightpearl for this *www.brightpearl.com*.

2. Be careful with commission sales

You may sell your products to larger organisations such as countywide craft bodies, who will then sell on the items to the public. If you're going to do this, make sure the rate of commission they keep on the sales is fair, and that the interim buyer pays you on time. Don't be caught out by big companies who may pay "low and slow".

3. Beware of VAT registration if you sell to the public

If you're selling your goods directly to the public, for example via your own website, don't register for VAT unless and until you have to (see *www.hmrc.gov.uk/vat*), because to the public, VAT just represents an increase on the cost of your product.

4. Save money where you can

As discussed earlier in this chapter, if your business won't take up much space, start from home and find out whether you can you save money by buying large items for your business second-hand? For example, if you want to make pottery, could you find a potter's wheel for sale on eBay or Gumtree, or even pay to use the wheel at your local art college, rather than buy a new one? But choose your cost savings wisely – see point 5.

5. Choose suppliers carefully

When you're thinking of how much you should pay for stock, don't just look for the cheapest option. Think also of quality and ease of acquisition. For example, it may be cheaper to buy your buttons for your homemade childrenswear from abroad, but if they break when tugged by a child, that's bad news for your brand and you could lose business. And there could be myriad reasons (stray ash clouds, political upheavals) why your imported stock can't reach you. There may be import tax too, which would push up the total price paid, so choose your suppliers carefully.

6. Think about how much stock you should buy in at a time

Suppliers may well give a discount if you buy a larger quantity, and you'll save on postage too, but make sure you don't end up with a pile of unsellable stock, which will put a dent in your profit and tie up cash. Your stock might not be perishable, but if you're making fabric bags and you buy a large quantity of bright orange material, will bright orange stay in fashion long enough for you to make the bags and sell them?

7. Work out your profitable lines

If you sell more than one kind of product, for example both hand-knitted mittens and scarves, it's a good idea to know which lines bring in the most profit, as that's where you should look to focus your time.

To work out how profitable each line is, take your sale price per unit of that item (for example, £10 per pair of mittens), then subtract how much each unit costs to make.

Some points to consider are:

★ Make sure you include *all* your costs. For example, if you're making patchwork cushions, think of not only the fabric and thread but also the cushion pad and zip, and don't forget to include your time for cutting out and sewing up. The more intricate the design, the longer this will take.

★ Use a spreadsheet to help you.

Ideally do this before you set your prices to customers, because it can be very hard to put prices up right away.

8. Set your prices carefully for handmade goods

How much premium can you charge for handmade goods? For example, if you are making bespoke cross-stitch wedding samplers then your customers will expect these to be sewn by hand, and will expect to pay a premium because this will take you a long time. But if you're making clothes then these would usually be machine-stitched, which would not take as long to make as handsewn garments.

9. Your website or mine?

Should you sell through your own website or through sites such as Etsy or Alibaba? In terms of costs, weigh up the price of building your own site (possibly by using a dedicated e-commerce platform such as Powa) or having it built by a professional, against the greater pool of customers you'll find through Etsy but will pay fees for. And don't forget that if you go through your own website you'll also have to invest time marketing the site and maintaining it, or pay someone to do that for you.

10. **Plan for the future**

No matter how small your business is, it's very important to plan and forecast your sales, costs, profit, and cash coming in and out. This isn't just for large businesses. You won't be able to keep everything in your head no matter how small your business is so write it down and record it!

Emily Coltman is Chief Accountant to FreeAgent Centraland author of
Finance for Small Business | *www.brightwordpublishing.com/finance*

FUNDING

Following the budgeting steps in this chapter will certainly help your finances, but if you think you'll need funding all the same, there are a few places you can look.

Friends and family

Friends and family are people you can trust – and asking them for money hopefully won't come with strings attached! Do consider having a written agreement, though, that covers the amount borrowed and a payback schedule, so that both parties are fully aware of exactly what has been agreed.

Fund101

If you need a bit of extra cash to get started or you're running a small business and need up to £500 to buy equipment, promotion flyers, hardware, etc., apply to Enterprise Nation's Fund 101.

Apply for between £50 and £500 via the website, outlining how much money you need and for what purpose. Make a good case for your idea and then encourage as many people as possible to vote for you. The number of votes required is equal to the amount of funding you're looking for, so to obtain £500 you'll need to secure 500 virtual votes. Make the most of your blog and social media accounts to encourage people to vote for you. You could also include a small note or flyer in parcels you send out explaining what you're asking people to do and how the money will make a difference to you and your business.

Once the money is received, it doesn't have to be paid back; it's for you to use on your idea or business, so an ideal way of giving your business a boost or getting that all important piece of equipment to take business to the next level.

Fund101 is supported by PayPal and Intuit and delivered by Enterprise Nation.

Apply via the website *www.enterprisenation.com/fund101*.

Emma Maudsley of Sock Monkey Emporium needed funds to invest in stylish business cards for the Oscars (yes, really!) and a camera so she could take professional shots of her products. Here's how she secured it …

Talent into turnover

NAME: EMMA MAUDSLEY
TALENT: CRAFTS
BUSINESS: SOCK MONKEY EMPORIUM

"I thought my life could be more effective with monkeys," says Emma Maudsley wryly. "I was working full time managing a coffee shop and I'm a single mum raising two kids. Every night it was get home, put the kids to bed, make a sock monkey then go to bed myself. Then do it all again the next day.

"There was no quality of life," the founder of the Sock Monkey Emporium in Lancaster declares. "There's this ethos that you can do it all, but I thought 'Hang on a minute!' So I decided to give up my job and make monkeys full time. I'm not making a fortune, but it's picking up every day."

Emma's commitment to monkeys (and assorted other colourful creatures) is proving to be a fruitful decision. Though she only started making sock monkeys in July 2010, she's already supplying two shops, shipping monkeys all over the world ("It's just normal now," she remarks) and doing in-store demonstrations for Hobbycraft. Emma's also due to make an appearance at the Oscars – or, at least, her business card is. This is where Fund101 came in.

"I'm a member of The Artisan Group, based in America," Emma explains. "They promote artisans across the world and they participate in the GBK Gift Lounges held prior to big awards ceremonies. That's where nominees and other celebrities are invited to come along and meet the sponsors and organisers who then gift them items – usually an example of their products.

> "The Artisan Group gift 'swag bags' come complete with handcrafted items made by an array of artisans. They've just done the GBK Emmys Gift Lounge and they're now doing events before the Golden Globes and the Oscars. My business cards will go into the swag bags given by The Artisan Group at the GBK Oscars Gift Lounge. My lowly little business card will get picked out and they'll say, 'That's good. I'd like a monkey'.

> "That's why they need to have an impact," she adds. "I'm hoping to get them done with a felt finish so they are quite tactile and feel different from the other business cards."

Emma also plans to spend some of the £500 she received from Fund101 on a camera to take good product shots for online marketplaces such as Etsy and Facebook. "A lot of people on Etsy have very professional-looking shots," she notes. "If you want to sell big league, you need to look like you can compete!"

It's not just monkeys she'll be photographing either. "I made six giraffes yesterday. I make cats, rabbits, anything really. I've even made a camouflage squid – I had to work out how to get eight long legs out a sock … "

But that's another story. For Emma, whose enterprise started as a source of extra income to raise money for a car, monkeys really have made her life more effective. "Now I get to take my daughters to school and meet all the other mums in the playground," she says cheerily. "And I get to spend time with my kids after school. I'm a lot happier for it."

How Emma secured her Fund101 votes

"It was predominantly Facebook," she explains. "And I've got just over 400 Twitter followers, too. The Artisan Group were very helpful and a lot voted for me. I asked mums in the school playground, people at craft fairs. I'm involved in guiding, too, so I asked people there."

The bank

High street banks are pretty eager to attract small business owners. Make the most of their enthusiasm and ask to speak to a small business advisor at your local branch. Take a copy of your business plan with you and be prepared to talk through it – remember, be clear about what your business does and explain how you can make money from it. It may help to run through this with a friend or colleague beforehand so that you feel prepared when you come to meet the advisor at the bank.

Credit cards

Many a business has been started with help from a flexible friend, but you must shop for the best rates. It's a competitive market and the credit card companies are keen for your business. Make sure you are on time with repayments (to avoid penalty interest charges) and aim to pay back the credit as soon as you can and as sales start coming in. This route is suggested based on start-up costs being small and the ability to pay back at speed so avoiding monthly repayments at high interest rates.

TIP: A clear division

It is a good idea to open a business bank account early on so you don't mix up your business and personal finances, which may complicate record keeping. To open a bank account you'll need to provide details of your business, a business plan and a certificate of incorporation for limited companies. Find out more about bank account opening requirements on the Business Link website: *bit.ly/hh3war*

Grants

There are grants available from a number of sources, including the government, European Union, local authorities and some charitable organisations, such as the Prince's Trust.

Find out more about grants and other help that may be available to you at:

* Business Link | *www.businesslink.gov.uk/grants*

* National Enterprise Network (with links to your local enterprise agency) | *www.nationalenterprisenetwork.org*

* The Prince's Trust (funds available to help young people start a business) | *www.princes-trust.org.uk*

* PRIME (offers a Zopa-PRIME Olderpreneur Loan) | *www.primebusinessclub.com*

* J4b Grants (grants, loans and venture capital) | *www.j4bgrants.co.uk*

Crowd funding

Crowd funding is a relatively recent development that involves sourcing funds from a group of others, with each lending a proportion of the total you wish to borrow. Check out *www.zopa.com* or *www.crowdcube.com* where you can secure a loan from people willing to lend.

Investors

Angel investors and venture capitalists can help raise large amounts of start-up funding or development capital for businesses looking to grow. It might be an idea to consider this route further down the line. It doesn't have to be a gruesome experience, though (à la *Dragons' Den*) as there are plenty of funds and investors out there who are eager to invest their money in good ideas. Unlike banks, investors will be looking for equity, i.e. part ownership in your business, in return for the funds.

★ Angels Den | *www.angelsden.co.uk*

★ Funding Circle | *www.fundingcircle.com*

★ British Business Angels Association | *www.bbaa.org.uk*

Chapter Six

Selling

SELL, SELL, SELL!

You have your idea. It's supported by research and a plan pointing you in the right direction. You've sorted out all the technology you need to get going. And with the company registered and admin/finances in shape, it's time to get into business by making some noise and getting sales!

In this section we'll look at how you achieve sales by selling offline and online, via platform sites and then via your own site.

Follow these five steps to making offline sales.

1. Make a list (check it twice)

Draw on your existing resources, grab your address book and circle the friends, family, colleagues and acquaintances you think might be interested in your product or service. Add to the list with details of local people and businesses.

2. Pitch up

Write to the people on your list and announce your new business venture. Consider this an opportunity to make your pitch, but don't be too pushy. And remember to address each recipient personally. No one likes a group email!

3. Follow up

Follow up in a few days time, either with another email or, better still, a phone call. Take some soundings as to the success of your pitch and react accordingly. If the potential customer or client sounds keen, go for it! Arrange to meet him or her to show your product or explain more about your service.

4. Meet up

Arrange a time and place to meet that's convenient for your potential customer or client. Be professional, but also likeable. They're equally important characteristics when making a sale.

If the customer agrees the deal, bring the meeting to a fairly speedy end. Your job is done – for now. It's time to head home and deliver on the promise you made with your first customer.

5. Make some noise

Once you've made your first sale – shout about it! If your new customer or client agrees, include them in a press release or write about them on your website or blog, so other potential customers or clients can see that you're well and truly in business!

TIP: Sales are flying high

Have promotional flyers made to take to events or deliver through doors. Increase your chances of turning flyers into firm sales by:

* having a design that is memorable, possibly quirky and, ideally, that your potential customers will want to keep on their desktop/in their purse/atop the kitchen shelf

* making the offer clear and confirming the benefits of buying

* including a call to action, i.e. a way in which the interested customer can contact you.

Promotional flyers

Getting your message to as many people as possible is key. Flyers are a cheap and quick way to do this. Stationery stores can normally print about 1,000 A5 flyers in half an hour while you wait – or simply pick them up later to suit you; a cost-effective way to get your brand in front of people.

TIP: Smile and dial

When making a sales call, do so standing up and smiling. To the person on the other end, you will come across as positive and confident about your product or service.

Talent into turnover

NAME: HELEN FIELD
TALENT: WILDLIFE
BUSINESS: ROUND ROBIN GARDEN WILDLIFE SUPPLIES

While she was watching the birds in her garden empty their feeders one day, Helen Field knew she would soon have to make yet another 20-mile round trip to her nearest garden centre to stock up on bird food, and it occurred to her that this must be an impossible task for the less mobile. She was struck with the idea of setting up her own business delivering garden wildlife supplies to people in her area and Round Robin Garden Wildlife Supplies was born.

Now the Round Robin customised van is a regular sight on the Cambridgeshire lanes. Helen delivers products including a wide range of birdseed sold by the kilo, Bill Oddie's Bird Food Recipes, nest boxes and feeders to customers within a 30-mile radius of her home.

As part of her business, Helen also offers a free bird feeder-filling service to the elderly and less mobile.

As Helen has been a keen wildlife enthusiast since she was a child, she is very keen that her business should also educate people about the wildlife in their garden, and so she decided to sell identification guides and also offers advice about the best foods for different species of birds.

Helen has big plans for the future and hopes to start selling cottage garden plants that attract a wide variety of bees, butterflies and insects and would also like to look into franchising opportunities for her business.

Top tip

Helen's top tip for wildlife lovers is to use as many different varieties of food as you can to attract a wider range of birds into your garden. You should also provide food and water all year round. In terms of business, Helen says, "Research your market thoroughly and put plenty of planning and groundwork in before you start turning your hobby into a business."

★ *www.round-robin.co.uk*

SELLING INTO PHYSICAL STORES

Maybe you've started by selling products direct to customers at craft shows but what about making sales via local shops?

Before you approach any shops, make a list of appropriate places where you think your product could work well. For example, does your town have a gift shop or art gallery, are there lots of boutiques that stock a range of different items? It's a good idea here to think outside the box, for example could your local coffee shop stock some of your items?

There are a huge range of potential stores you can sell your work to – especially if you think outside the box

5 top tips for market placement

Laura Rigney, founder of PitcherHouse and Mumpreneur UK, is author of *Pitching Products for Small Business* and offers her five top tips for pitching your product effectively (*www.brightwordpublishing.com/pitchingproducts*).

1. Be confident with pricing

Selling in wholesale is a whole new ballpark as far as pricing is concerned. Make your product attractive to buyers with your pricing. A great way to show you're trying to help retailers is to setup a structured pricing system, i.e. 100 units or less £xx per unit, 101-500 units £xx per unit and 501 units or more £xx per unit. This system could also encourage shops and buyers to place larger orders.

2. Understand your product inside out

This means technical data as well as knowing why someone would buy it. When you get a meeting with a buyer or approach a shop owner, talk with confidence about where the product is made, by who, and using what kind of materials. Remember there is pressure on large retailers to "go green", so the more you can offer that as a potential supplier the more attractive you will be.

3. Be prepared

If a buyer places an order, how quickly will you have manufacturing, distribution and storage in place? Buyers won't expect a new small business to have a giant factory sitting waiting for someone to press the "go" button but they will want a realistic estimate of how long it will be until your product is in their warehouses/on the shop shelf. Once you have given your timings, stick to them. Even if this means exaggerating the time it will take for them to be delivered. Better to be early rather than late!

4. Pitch perfect

If you're pitching in person, make it informative, exciting and interesting and where possible have evidence of past sales and customer satisfaction. You need to know your figures without having to look through paperwork and be prepared to haggle a little on prices. If someone likes your product enough and you have sold it well enough they will buy it even if it's a few pennies more than they would like to pay. In the other direction, sometimes it may be worth offering a larger than normal discount as a trial for their first order.

5. Stay listed

When a company takes on your product it's called being listed. Once you are listed the work is just beginning! It is now time to stay listed for as long as possible and the way to do this is through marketing and PR. The more you promote your product and the shops/galleries/boutiques that are selling them, the more they will be bought by consumers thus encouraging buyers to place more orders with you!

Laura Rigney is author of Pitching Products for Small Business

SELLING ONLINE

A presence on other sites

Raise profile and make sales via powerful platform sites before creating your own. Whether selling boutique crafts or business concepts, there are a number of options and the upside is these sites attract customers on your behalf, and some of them attract customers from all over the world. Here are a number of websites that enable you to sell.

> *You can easily raise your profile and sales via platform sites*

eBay

eBay has grown to become the largest shopping mall on the web. In 2010 there were 160,000 registered businesses trading on the site in the UK, generating sales of £1.6 billion a year. The good thing is, having a store on eBay means you are opened up to an international audience and many potential customers!

★ *www.eBay.co.uk*

TIP: eBay advice

eBay expert, Dan Wilson, offers 5 tips on how to make the most of the mega marketplace known as eBay:

1. Start small

Go slow until you've found your way. Start with a few, easy-to-post items and learn about eBay before boosting your range and prices. Don't stake too much on your first eBay bet.

2. Sell like you mean it

The eBay marketplace is competitive and you'll lose out unless you have top-notch listings. Craft fabulous item titles, make impeccable pictures and write descriptions that tempt buyers. Be truthful and honest and look professional from the start.

3. Be quick off the mark

Buyers have come to expect great service. Dispatch orders quickly — preferably within 24 hours of payment — and well packed, and make sure you reply to emails and other communications swiftly, too. The quality and speed of your replies and dispatches has an impact on customer feedback.

4. Put a lid on postal costs

Understand postage and packaging costs and make sure you factor it in to your costs where necessary.

5. Loyalty means profit

When you're building your eBay business, encouraging repeat buyers is important. Once a buyer trusts you as an online seller, they're likely to keep coming back. Offer discounts and incentives with every dispatch and cross-market complementary products.

Dan Wilson is an eBay expert and author of Make Serious Money on eBay UK, *www.wilsondan.co.uk*

Enterprise Nation

Whether you're a web designer, accountant or marketer, the Enterprise Nation marketplace connects your business services with business buyers. We refer to it as the friendliest business-to-business marketplace on the web. You can list your business in the directory from just £5 per month. It's supported by a business blog, with tips and advice on sales and marketing, IT efficiency, productivity and motivation, and a community for all the help and support you need to start and grow your business.

★ *www.enterprisenation.com* | @e_nation

Alibaba.com

Having a presence on this site enables you to buy and sell and source supplies with companies from across the globe. The site has visitors from 240 countries and regions, with over 1 million registered users in the UK. Through the site you can locate suppliers or make sales of your finished product direct to customers. Alibaba.com is a champion of international trade; carrying out research on the topic, providing a platform for traders to interact, and promoting overseas sales as a form of business that is wholly viable, regardless of company size.

★ *www.alibaba.com* | @AlibabaTalk_UK

Amazon Marketplace

You may be used to buying from Amazon, but have you considered the site as a platform from which to sell? Have your products appear before millions of customers all around the world by signing up to Amazon Marketplace. It offers two sales options: a package for casual sellers who expect to sell less than 35 items a month (a fixed fee per sale plus a referral fee), and for more seasoned sellers there is the 'sell a lot' package, which has a monthly charge plus a referral fee for unlimited sales that do not have to be in the Amazon catalogue.

★ *www.amazon.co.uk/marketplace*

iStockphoto

Want to sell your photography, illustrations, videos or music effects around the world? This is the site for you:

> "iStockphoto is the web's original source for royalty-free stock images, media and design elements. For over 10 years artists, designers and photographers from all over the world have come here to create, work and learn."

To start selling, all you have to do is join the site, apply to be a contributor and submit samples of your work. As a contributor, you receive a base royalty rate of 20% for each file downloaded, which goes up to 40% if you exclusively display work on the site.

★ *www.istockphoto.com*

HANDMADE MARKETPLACES

A growing number of sites are dedicated to helping the artisan and handmade business owner sell goods across the globe.

Etsy | *www.etsy.com*

"The world's handmade marketplace" (and a great place to start your selling)

How does it work?

1. You list the item on Etsy for a fee. It costs 20 cents (roughly 12p) to list an item for four months.

2. Shoppers then find your item, and purchase it from you directly, using your payment system which you have set up with Etsy, for example PayPal. Etsy takes a 3.5% transaction fee from the total sale price of each sale.

3. You then ship the item directly to your customer.

Getting started

Setting up a shop on Etsy is easy and should only take a few minutes: *www.etsy.com/join*

You will need to enter your Etsy username here, which will be displayed to customers looking at your products. Remember to think about your branding and how you want to present yourself to potential customers when entering these details.

Paying fees

All of your fees will be paid using the credit card you list when you register, or the PayPal account you link to your Etsy account. Etsy will calculate your fees on a monthly basis and email you with a list of payments that are due. You can also pay your bill manually through your account.

Community

Etsy has a thriving community where sellers, artists and creators all come together to share their work and ideas with one another. Etsy also run events such as Craft Nights, which could be a great way to meet other crafters and promote your products to a receptive audience.

The site has a blog which highlights new product launches and new initiatives, plus featured sellers and debates on various topics.

Forums feature strongly on the site, so if you need advice, look here as there will always be someone who can help you find what you need!

Etsy have recently launched a free eBook called *Getting Started on Etsy* to guide you through the process of becoming a seller. You can download a copy at *www.etsy.me/GettingStartedOnEtsy*.

Not On The High Street | *www.notonthehighstreet.com*

"One basket, hundreds of unique shops"

How does it work?

Not On The High Street offers you the chance to promote and sell your product under the umbrella of their brand and be supported by their in-house team. They look after all of the e-commerce, administration and marketing elements of selling through the site, so all you need to worry about are the products.

Not On The High Street differs from a number of other platform sites in that they are very selective about who sells with them and decline over 90% of applications. Membership packages vary but the basic package allows you to add 30 products to your own store, with your own logo, company name and URL.

Getting started

If you're interested in getting set up with NOTHS, the first thing you will need to do is to take some photographs of your products and submit these using the online application form.

Applications can take up to seven working days to be processed. After that time you will be contacted by a member of the team.

Folksy | *www.folksy.com*

"Folksy is a place to buy handmade things, and for makers to sell their work and find supplies. Based in the UK, Folksy aims to reclaim craft and showcase talented makers and their work."

Interestingly, you can sell craft supplies on Folksy as well as handmade goods, so long as they are listed as 'supplies' and not in the 'handmade' category.

How does it work?

1. You list the item on Folksy for a fee. It costs 20p to list an item for 180 days or until the item is sold.

2. Shoppers find your item and purchase it from you directly, using your payment system which you have set up with Folksy, for example PayPal, or you can accept other payments, such as cash or cheque at your own discretion. Folksy takes a 5% commission fee from the total value of each sale.

3. You then ship the item directly to your customer.

Getting started

The first thing you need to do is to decide on the username for your shop. This can't be changed so think carefully about your branding and how you want to appear to prospective customers.

Once your item is listed, customers can start viewing and purchasing. When an order is received you will get an order from Folksy with all the buyer's details and the information about the product ordered. You will also receive an email from PayPal to say payment has been completed. You then ship the product directly to the customer.

Paying fees

You settle fees through the Your Account section of the website. The total shown will be made up of billed and unbilled fees as well as the 5% commission on sales.

Community

Folksy features a blog which gives updates on important news and events. The site also has a forum where members can discuss craft tips, as well as events, ideas for your shopfront and anything else that takes your fancy!

iCraft | *www.icraft.co.uk*

"Creativity without borders"

How does it work?

1. First you need to set up an account with iCraft which costs CAD$25. This is a one-off fee to register and ensure your identity.

2. You then decide on which membership package you would like from the following:

   * 1 to 5 products – free but advertising will appear at the bottom of your page

   * Starter (5 to 50 items) – CAD$5.00/month. Every additional item is CAD$0.20/month.

   * Professional (5 to 100 items) – CAD$10.00/month. Every additional item is CAD$0.20 /month.

   * Elite (Unlimited items) – CAD$15.00/month

2. Shoppers find your item and place an order. iCraft will process all payments through PayPal and notify you of the payment deposit. You don't pay any commission to iCraft for this, or for the sale of the product.

3. You ship the item directly to your customer.

Getting started

You can set up your shop with iCraft here – *www.icraft.ca/registration.php*

Community

iCraft features the Handmade Community where members get together to share their love of all things handmade. The community features message boards to discuss ideas, share tips and generally support each other, while Blog Central publishes helpful articles and topical news.

DaWanda | *en.dawanda.com*

"DaWanda is the place for unique and individual products and people. Buy handmade and hard to find goods, share your discoveries with your friends and create your own collections."

How does it work?

List your items on the site and set up your own shop which gives you the option of a direct URL – nice and easy to promote to your customers!

People will browse your listings and when someone orders a product you receive an email. You check the details of the order, making a note of any special requests from the buyer, and once happy to go ahead you click to confirm the order, so the buyer can see the final price and pay you. You then ship the item directly to the customer using the method you have specified in the listing.

Getting started

With DaWanda you can set up your own shop for free – all you need to do is provide a name and set up 20 shop categories. You can create your own shop window at this stage to show off the key items in your shop. As soon as this has been set up, you can start listing your items and selling to customers!

DaWanda also features something called the DaWanda widget, which is a tool for displaying your shop on your own website or blog.

Paying fees

DaWanda charges a 5% commission on all sales but does not charge for listing products. Once your fees reach a minimum of EUR5.00, DaWanda will email you an invoice with instructions on how to pay.

Community

The website features the News Bulletin Board as well as a blog, ideal for getting all the latest information on what DaWanda offers and what's popular on the site. The forums are a great place to chat with other crafters and there are also video, social media and Gift Detective areas.

Artfire | *www.artfire.com*

"The Premier handmade marketplace to buy and sell handmade crafts, supplies, vintage and art."

How does it work?

Set up your shop and list as many items as you want, with up to 10 photographs per item.

The customer will browse your shop and place an order. You receive the customer's payment and also their delivery details in order to ship the product.

Getting started

You can set up your shop for free at – *www.artfire.com/ext/register/account*

You then pay nothing for 30 days, and after that the rate is a £7.56 a month for unlimited listings. Artfire do not take a commission on sales.

Paying fees

Fees will be taken from your nominated payment card on the same day each month (the one on which you originally signed up). For example, if you joined on the 5th December, you would be charged your monthly fee on the 5th of every month.

Community

Artfire has a range of different community options for you to get involved in and interact with other members. There are forums where you can communicate and share ideas with other crafters, as well as ArtDaily, which is an opportunity to learn new crafts and get sound business advice, plus there's the chance to join a guild and earn a guild badge, as well as listen to the weekly podcast from John Jacobs and Tony Ford, giving tips on how to promote your business and use Artfire to its full potential.

MISI (Make It, Sell It) | *www.misi.co.uk*

"The home of buying and selling handmade in the UK."

How does it work?

Create a shop with Misi and list your items for free. Customers can then browse through your shop and purchase items. When you sell a product you will receive an email notification from Misi which will prompt you to log in to see the full details of the sale. Payment can either be by cheque or PayPal, and once payment is received, you ship the product direct to the customer.

Paying fees

Misi charges 20p per listing, which will be added to your account as soon as you start listing items. Misi also take a 3% commission fee on every sale and this is also added to your account. Fees are then payable on a monthly basis.

Community

The Misi community section is broken down into several areas including: a blog where crafters write about their latest ideas, materials and events; a forum for sharing tips and ideas; and a Meet the Maker section where shop-owners and crafters are encouraged to share their experiences with the community.

ShopHandmade | *www.shophandmade.com*

"Rewarding Creativity."

How does it work?

You can sell your items in five easy steps! Once you have listed your products, customers can browse them and begin buying right away.

When an item sells you will be notified by email, and payment will be made to your registered PayPal account. You then ship the item using the easy-to-print labels through PayPal.

Getting started

To get started firstly, you need to list your item for a small fee of 25 cents, and then upload up to five photos per item. Then you need to decide if you are participating in Sales and Galleries and activate your listing.

When you are listing items, there is also the opportunity to get the listing sponsored, which means a third-party sponsor will pay for listing your item, costing you nothing. There are several sponsors to choose from and their sponsorship simply means that a non-intrusive advertisement will appear on your product page.

Paying fees

ShopHandmade only charge a percentage of the item's final selling price if you have chosen to do this. The payment is taken when the item actually sells.

Community

ShopHandmade features blogs from various sellers so that you can see what other crafters are up to and keep track of developments and new ideas in the crafting world.

LOOK AT ME!

Increase the chances of having your products browsed and bought by uploading quality photos of your items. Successful eBay sellers Mark and Philomena have seen first-hand the power of having professional images and how this translates into sales. With this experience, they have set up a new company – Business Photography – to help you take your best shot:

There are basically two options for producing images of product: Do it Yourself or Bring in a Professional.

DIY – The seller of single small items

If you are selling single items below a value of £100, you should be taking your own pictures. Why? Simply because your profit margin will not soak up the cost of a professional commercial photographer whose prices are typically going to range from £15 to £20 for a single image (lower for multiples).

Whilst you will not be able to equal the image quality that a professional provides, you will be able to supply acceptable quality images if you invest in a good basic setup.

Our recommendation for equipment

★ A bridge camera with macro and minimum 10mp (Fuji make some good bridge cameras, £200-£300) and a good tripod (£80)

★ A light tent (purchase the largest you can fit on a table – 100cm cubed is a good size for small to medium sized product, £25-£40 should get a decent quality tent)

★ Continuous lights with stands (daylight balanced) – with as much power as you can afford (more light = faster shutter speeds), expect to pay £200 for about 2400w of light

★ An image editor like Lightroom 3 which will enable you to batch process images quickly – £220 (you could use Gimp which is free but it will not be as quick with batch processing we imagine)

★ A decent computer that can handle lots of images being edited at once – minimum spec: Windows 7, 4 gig of ram, decent processor and an external drive for storage of the images

★ Preferably – an area dedicated to photography, so that your setup is ready for use continuously

Setup

★ Choose a mid-tone grey background for the backdrop in your tent. White backgrounds (pure white) are very hard to achieve and takes professional-level skills, whereas a mid-tone is forgiving and will give a background to contrast a light or dark item against enabling high turnover of images produced

★ Do not use bright colours as your background as they produce strong colour casts; white should look white, a red background will make white look pink

★ Remove/blank all sources of light other than the daylight bulb lighting, this stops lots of lighting problems

★ Set your lights so that you have one shining on top of the tent and two to one side to create some contrast in the tent

★ Set your camera to its auto mode with macro and shoot in JPEG

★ When taking the images think about your framing of the image, get it right in the camera so that you don't need to crop it afterwards using software

★ Keep your setup consistent and your images will remain consistent

★ Bulk edit in Lightroom and make sure that when you export your images you reduce them to a standard web resolution size (640 x 640 is a good middle ground we feel)

Bring in the professional – the seller of multiple quantity items

Have you ever heard the saying that "accountants pay for themselves"? A professional commercial photographer does the very same thing; they produce images that help you sell your product because they know how to portray quality and professionalism. They invest substantial sums to deliver this level of quality through equipment and knowledge.

The cost of producing the images will be proportionally small to the sales attached to that image; one image for £20 that helps sell 300 items is not expensive.

Quality of image helps differentiate between competitors – look at the competition, how good are their images? Now compare yourselves to them. Examine the market leaders and the trendy e-commerce giants who tend to invest in high quality images.

The type of seller that should use professional help will probably be selling cross platform on many sites and be handling large ranges of stock and will be looking for growth.

The images produced should fill certain criteria:

* Pure white background – the industry standard in the majority of cases

* High contrast and colour-corrected images (eBay are considering using contrast in images as a factor in Best Match –third party platform companies like you to have good images)

* Consistent images – using stock images from different suppliers will result in inconsistent quality, lighting and backgrounds and usually the images are small and therefore of poor quality when expanded

* Branding in the form of subtle watermarking can again be used to support marketing as can your consistent style

Finding a professional commercial photographer

* Ascertain their skill-set in this niche area of commercial photography – they should have a website with examples of their product shots which you can examine

* Understand what they provide for the price, and make sure basic colour correction, white balancing and removal of flaws is included – you do not want to be handed half-finished images that need more money spending on them to make them usable

* Find a specialist in commercial photography – a wedding photographer will not be equipped to supply commercial product photography as a rule, neither will the "friend" with a camera

Making sure your products look their best is a must

* Make sure that the photographer has the equipment to shoot on your premises if you have large runs as this will reduce transport costs

* Negotiate price discounts if you are requesting hundreds of images

We hope that helps your thoughts in this area and you find this a good introductory guide. If you need help or advice on this subject please feel free to contact Mark or Philomena at Business Photography.

* *www.business-photography.biz*

Content adapted and with permission from a post originally appearing on Tamebay (www.tamebay.com)

Talent into turnover

NAME: TRACEY MATHIESON
TALENT: FLORISTRY
BUSINESS: FOXTAIL LILLY

Tracey Mathieson's business, Foxtail Lilly, has grown from small beginnings and has blossomed into a successful business.

The seeds were sown over 15 years ago when Tracey moved back to the family cottage after completing a degree in photography at the University of Nottingham, and working briefly as a photographer, to look after her father who had unfortunately become ill. "He grew up here and I was born here. My grandparents used to be coal merchants and the barn we converted into the shop was where they kept the trap for deliveries," Tracey says. She took a job at a local herb farm in Brigstock and her love of gardening began to take root.

"I tend to get quite obsessive about things – first photography, then plants. I enrolled on an RHS evening class and began looking after other people's gardens. Later I worked for Miriam Rothschild at the Ashton Estate, where I learnt a lot about wild varieties."

Several years ago, she began dividing up plants from her garden and selling them outside the 18th century cottage with bunches of sweet peas, snapdragons, old-fashioned roses and fragrant lavenders. Encouraged by the positive reaction, Tracey and her friend Sue Kirk, who sells woven willow sculptures, took a stall at Oundle farmers' market. The reaction was positive: "People really seemed to like the combination of simple country flowers and crafts, and the idea of setting up a shop in the barn seemed a natural progression – we knew we had a loyal following," Tracey remembers.

However, Tracey knew that she would need more than the flowers from her garden to create a viable business and so began to make trips to Newark antiques fair to hunt for vintage china, gardenalia, enamelware, small armoires, cupboards and mirrors.

Alongside this, Tracey networked with local craftspeople to source hand-sewn cushions, cards and rustic handicraft, which are also sold in the shop. Tracey says her look has to be natural and not regimented and this is shown in the arrangements of all these elements in her barn. The stock is always changing as she constantly searches for perfect vintage pieces to include.

Continuing the tradition of her grandparents, the shop remains essentially a family affair with husband Rick helping with deliveries and daughter Poppy serving on Saturdays.

Tracey has been very pro-active about marketing and as well as handing out fliers at the local farmers' markets and in her local, she regularly opens her beautiful garden to intrigued visitors. She also hosts seasonal shopping days saying, "Every extra element helps bring more people through the door."

Her plans for the future include turning another of her stables into a workshop where she can prepare flowers for weddings, as well as run classes for others.

Top tip

"My photography skills have come in very handy for advertising my business. I make postcards of flower photos to sell or hand out, and I have made a book of my wedding photos to show clients. Use your other skills and incorporate them in your business.

Another idea is to have special events or days to create interest in your business and your products."

★ *www.foxtail-lilly.co.uk*

SALES VIA YOUR OWN SITE

You've started making sales via platform sites and feel it's time to create your own home on the web.

Home on the web, window to the world

Your site is a powerful marketing tool and a way to make money. Having the right technology and knowledge allows you to build, develop and maintain your site. And you can do it all in-house.

Let's look at the main ways to develop a professional looking online presence.

BLOGGING

Blogging is a website or part of a website that's regularly updated by an individual or a group of 'bloggers'. There are blogs on any number of topics and the fact that anyone can start blogging for free makes the medium diverse and exciting.

It's an easy way to get online, as you write posts on your topic of choice, upload images and video and become the go-to place for customers looking for your advice/tips/services/products.

Search engines love blogs and the more you write, the higher up the search-engine ranks you will go. Writing regularly is likely to lead to a loyal readership and it's an effective way to communicate your news with existing and potential customers.

Readers can add their comments to your entries if you allow them and you can use your blog to answer questions and establish yourself as an expert in your field. It's free and easy to get started. Try one of the services below.

* Blogger | *www.blogger.com*
* TypePad | *www.typepad.com*
* WordPress | *www.wordpress.com*

See page 148 for details on how to make money from your blog.

Now you see me

After getting to grips with blogging, why not try your hand at vlogging? This stands for video blogging and is an effective way to interact with customers who want to see you, your products and other happy customers. Vlogging expert, Niamh Guckian, offers tips on how to vlog like a pro.

Vlogging can help you tell people your story, using motion pictures and audio. It could be a demonstration of your crafty skills, an atmosphere piece about the place you go for ideas or an interview with a person who inspires you.

The gear

It's important to get to know your gear – whether using your phone or a fancy-cam, become an expert on your chosen camera.

Where possible use manual control with your camera – this applies to white balance, exposure and focus. Learn the rules and then have fun breaking them.

Use focus and depth of field to add style to your shooting. Using a tripod sets your work apart from amateur shooting and allows for good steady shot composition.

Safety

Using a small camera can make you feel like you can take risks that you wouldn't otherwise. This has advantages at times but don't take unnecessary risks. Don't shoot from rooftops or get into water!

Light

As a video-blogger, you will mostly be working with available or natural light. Try to get the most from what's available at the time.

Sound

Audio recording is a specialist art form. What we need to achieve as self-shooters is clean and non-distorted sound. Distorted audio is not fixable, and can usually be prevented.

Interviews

If your piece is interview-based, engage with the contributor, communicate with them and let them know clearly what you want them to do. Create an atmosphere where the contributor is comfortable, and make sure they know they can stop and start again, or ask questions.

Make sure the interview is a sequence, that it has a beginning, middle and end, and can stand alone if necessary.

Export and upload

Learn about the optimum settings and platforms for your finished piece.

Niamh Guckian is the Director of Totally Wired.

Make money from your website/blog

If your product is your website or blog, sell its content and/or parts of your online space. As traffic to your online home increases, so also do your chances of generating income. Make a profit from your posts with this top ten list of options.

1. Display advertising

Offer advertising on your site. The more niche your audience, the more likely you are to attract advertisers.

The information you'll need to provide includes:

* number of unique visitors

* number of impressions

* average duration of visit

* visitor demographics.

Write a basic rate card, add it to your site and send it to corporate marketing departments and media-buying agencies.

TIP: Show me your rates!

The purpose of a media rate card is to show potential advertisers what your site can deliver to them in terms of traffic and possible sales. To do this, include some key points:

* **A brief description of the site:** What it does and for whom.

* **Visitor demographics:** Do you have data on the age of your site visitors, their home region, gender, etc? If so, include it, as it helps build a picture of your audience.

* **Site traffic:** What are your unique visitor numbers and length of time spent on the site? Include a note or graph if the figures are increasing.

* **Costings:** Do you have a cost-per-click (CPC) or cost-per-impression (CPM) rate? If so, include it here, along with the price of other sponsorship options. Offer a menu but leave some flexibility, with 'costed on a project basis' for sponsor features that would benefit from a more tailored proposal.

* **Screen shots:** Showing how and where adverts or sponsored features appear on the site.

* **Media activity:** Note where you've recently been covered in the media, online and off, so that potential sponsors can see how and where you're promoting the site.

★ **Testimonials:** Positive comments from existing sponsors give credibility to you and confidence to the next potential sponsor.

★ **Team details:** Who are the faces behind the site and what are their credentials? In other words, your background career and activities, etc.

Round this off with your contact details so that anyone interested can get in touch and place an order!

2. Google AdSense

This tool from Google does the work for you in that it places relevant ads on your site and earns you money when people click on them. You can customise the appearance of the ads so they sit well with the style of your site.

★ *www.google.co.uk/adsense*

3. TextLinkAds

These ads offer direct click-throughs from text on your site. You submit your site to TextLinkAds and then upload the ad code provided. It's your choice whether you approve or deny the supplied ads. Once that's done, you start making money as visitors click on the ads. Try this and Skimlinks, which converts words on your site to affiliate links so that you earn from those, too.

★ *www.text-link-ads.com*

★ *www.skimlinks.com*

4. Sponsored conversations

Get paid for posts (and now tweets) with services like IZEA that match bloggers with advertisers. Some doubt the ethical stance of paying a blogger to write something about a product but there's no doubt that it's a money maker.

★ *www.izea.com*

5. Affiliate schemes

Sign up to affiliate schemes like the Amazon Associates programme, where you can earn up to 10% in referrals by advertising Amazon products. The programme works by driving traffic to Amazon.co.uk through specially formatted links. You earn referral fees on sales generated through those links. Monthly cheques are sent to you from Amazon and it's easy and free to join.

★ *affiliate-program.amazon.co.uk*

6. Sponsored features

This could include a host of options. Approach advertisers with suggestions of a sponsored eBook, e-news, podcast, webchat, poll or survey. These applications can be added to your site at a low cost yet generate good revenue. *See page 200 for details on how these features can help you become an expert in your field.* For:

★ eBook creation, try *www.blurb.com*

★ a survey or poll feature, try *www.surveymonkey.com*

★ email marketing, try *www.mailchimp.com*

7. Expert help

Offer your expertise and charge people to log on and watch or listen. This could be made available through:

Teleclasses

Invite customers and contacts to a call where you offer your expertise on a one-to-many basis.

GoToWebinar

Deliver a presentation to potentially thousands of paying customers via *www.gotowebinar.co.uk*.

8. Deals with suppliers

Do deals with suppliers. Hosting a travel blog? Agree a percentage each time a booking is made via your site. Hosting a shedworking blog? Create a directory that includes all garden office suppliers but with an enhanced listing for those who pay.

9. Turn a blog into a book

Follow the lead of Sue Hedges and Angela Savchenko who had their blog, Moan About Men (*www.moanaboutmen.com*), turned into a book which is now selling across the UK and acting as an effective marketing tool for the site!

10. Please donate

If you'd rather just ask for a small donation from your visitors, this is possible too via a donate feature from PayPal. Add a PayPal donate button to your site: *tinyurl.com/63swy9x*

Selling your products is obviously a great way to make money, but are there other avenues that you could explore that would complement this and would allow you to make some more income. Take a look at Chapter Ten for more information.

YOUR OWN WEBSITE

Create a home on the web through having your own website that you have built to your own requirements or by investing in a template website. Let's look at both options.

DIY

You have decided to build your own site or have a developer take care of it for you. The first thing to do is buy a domain, i.e. a URL. A domain makes up a part of your website and email address. For example, the domain name I own is *enterprisenation.com*. My website address is *www.enterprisenation.com* and my email address is *emma@enterprisenation.com*. Both use the *enterprisenation.com* domain name.

A domain isn't only your web address it's also a big part of your brand on the internet so think carefully when choosing one – although your options will be increasingly limited, since so many combinations have already been snapped up!

There are lots of domain registration companies whose websites allow you to check for available domain names and often suggest available alternatives. Here are three options.

* 1&1 | *www.1and1.co.uk*
* 123-reg | *www.123-reg.co.uk*

★ Easily.co.uk | *www.easily.co.uk*

Registering a domain name doesn't give you a website, just an address for it (and an email address). Think of it like reserving a car parking space. You've got the space, now you need to buy the car!

A hosting company will sort you out with the web space to host your website. This is measured in megabytes and gigabytes, just like the information on your computer. You upload the files that make up a website – pictures and pages – to this space, so that the rest of the world can see them.

In terms of how much web space you will need, basic hosting packages offer about 250MB of web space, but anything over 1 or 2GB is more sensible and it will also allow you to handle more traffic on your website as it grows more popular.

With a domain name and web space, potential customers should be able to type your website address into their browser and find out all about your business – just as soon as you've built your site. Finding a hosting company shouldn't be hard. Most domain registration companies, including those mentioned above, offer web space as a package and vice versa.

TIP: A website for free

In 2010, the Getting British Business Online (GBBO) project was launched by Google and offered free websites to 100,000 businesses. GBBO is growing by continuing to offer free websites and helping online businesses expand. Visit *www.gbbo.co.uk* and sign up for your own free website.

When it comes to hiring a designer, have a think about what you'd like your website to do for your business. The easiest way to start is to think of your website as a brochure, but remember to include the following pages at the very least.

* About us

* News

* Products or services

* FAQs (Frequently Asked Questions)

* Contact us

Choose a designer who has carried out work you like the look of and for companies in a similar kind of sector to your own. That way, the designer will understand what site you're after – and what your kind of visitor will be looking for, as well as how they like to browse and buy. Check out the Enterprise Nation marketplace (*www.enterprisenation.com*) or similar sites to find the right web designer for you.

See page 161 for details on how to integrate PayPal payments into your site and turn site content into commerce.

How to brief a web designer/developer

Here is Emily Hewett's (*www.birdsontheblog.co.uk*) advice on how best to brief a web designer/developer:

When working with a designer you need to have a coherent brief for them to follow. Here are my hints and tips to help you be clear in your mind what it is you want so you can communicate this to your designer and use the brief as a point of reference throughout the project.

Who are you? – even if the designer has worked with your organisation previously, always give them a short summary of your company; who you are and what you do. This will help refresh their memory and tune in to your particular industry sector. You will also need to tell them about your market and how you fit in to the larger scheme of things, for example who your competitors are both locally and nationally.

What do you want to achieve? – you need to detail the purpose, for example are you wanting to capture data, generate sales, increase footfall, etc.

Who are you talking to? – outline a profile of who your customer is. The designer will need to know whether they are targeting females, males or both, what is the age group of the audience, what is their average income and what's their location.

What tone are you using? – deciding on how you speak to your audience is important. You may be writing the copy yourself or you may have a copywriter to do this for you. In this section of the brief tell the designer if it's a laidback chatty tone or a formal, informative tone. The tone of the copy will affect the design and these two elements need to gel to produce a successful end product.

What are your likes and dislikes? – provide examples to the designer wherever possible of what you like or don't like online. It might be a certain colour palette or illustration style or it could be a format. Any of these things help the designer get into your head and understand what it is that you require, making for a better working relationship.

Are there any mandatory elements? – tell the designer if there are any mandatory fonts, colours, logos, legal text, images, etc. so that they can make sure they are producing something on brand that adheres to your corporate image.

What's your budget? – this doesn't need to be set in stone and a good designer won't take a large budget and fit a job to it, they should find the most cost-effective way of producing exactly what you want, but if you have a small budget the designer will have to make decisions based on what they can realistically achieve in that price bracket.

When do you want it? – make the designer aware of your ultimate deadline that needs to be achieved.

Have you covered everything? – show the brief to a colleague or friend to see if they understand the content and once happy with the brief, send or talk it through with your designer and invite questions so they are aware you are approachable and that you are both working from the same list of requirements.

Doing this not only creates a good bond between you and your designer, it also helps you clarify what you really want from your website.

Emily Hewett, Birds on the Blog (www.birdsontheblog.co.uk)

Template site

If DIY feels and sounds too much like hard work, there are a good number of companies offering template websites that come with domain registration, hosting, e-commerce and a basic level of design as part of the package.

There are a number of template site providers offering websites that can be set up today and trading by tomorrow. Check out these options:

* Moonfruit | *www.moonfruit.com*

* Create.net | *www.create.net*

* Magento | *www.magentocommerce.com*

TIP: Take care of the Ts and Cs

When building your site, include some basic terms and conditions. These will cover information about the site content and your policy on data privacy. View sample terms and conditions on the Business Link website: *bit.ly/csYSTz*

Five tips for making your website legally compliant

These tips are offered by Joanna Tall, founder of *OffToSeeMyLawyer.com*.

1. Display terms of use

Think of your website like a board game you are about to play with your visitors. They arrive and are ready to play and you need to state the rules or else it will be chaos! So, for example, state what they can and cannot do, e.g. may they copy your materials? May they rely on the information you provide without double-checking with you or elsewhere? What liability are you prepared to accept? Provide a link to your terms of use, ideally on every page of your website or under a 'Legals' section.

2. Display your privacy policy

Most websites collect personal data about their visitors either by getting them to register on the site or sign up for a newsletter. By law you must tell visitors what you will be doing with this data and the best way to do this is to set out the information in a so-called privacy policy. Again, a link to it on every page is best. More complex rules apply if you plan to collect sensitive information or information from children, or want to pass the information to third parties; for this you should consult a lawyer. Additionally, you are likely to need to register as a data processor under the Data Protection Act. Simply go to *www.ico.gov.uk* for more information.

3. If selling goods or services online, display your terms of sale

Just as with the board game example, you need rules for selling your goods or services. Most importantly, you need to get your visitors to acknowledge that they accept them. So ideally get them to tick a box stating that they accept them before they proceed to check out. You also need to draw their attention to their rights under the Distance Selling Regulations, e.g. cancellation rights amongst others.

See page 163 for details of the Distance Selling Regulations.

4. Protect your copyright in the website content

Although you automatically own the copyright in the content that you create, best practice is to remind your visitors! Say, for example, "Copyright 2011 Lawyers R Great Ltd" and if your logo or name is trademarked, broadcast the fact! After all, you will have spent a lot of money in getting it that far and it will enhance your brand in the market.

5. State who you are!

By law you need to state a full postal address and contact number and if you are a limited company, the company's registered address, number and country of registration. This also applies to your emails, so add these details to your signature.

Joanna Tall is founder of www.offtoseemylawyer.com, where most terms and conditions can be bought from the 'oven ready' document shop.

E-COMMERCE TOOLS

Open your website up to sales by adding a shopping cart or plugging in an e-commerce tool. Here are some suggestions.

Shopping carts

Add a shopping cart to make life easy for your visitors to click and buy. Check out the shopping cart providers below.

* GroovyCart | *www.groovycart.co.uk*

* Zen Cart | *www.zen-cart.com*

* RomanCart | *www.romancart.com*

* osCommerce | *www.oscommerce.com*

* CubeCart | *www.cubecart.com*

* Frooition | *www.frooition.com* (shopping cart and full website)

Research the product that suits you best, taking into account hosting provision, back-end admin, and built-in search engine optimisation.

Plugging in

If you are blogging and want to start selling, consider these plug-in tools that could turn browsers into buyers.

★ WordPress e-Commerce shopping cart – "suitable for selling your products, services, and or fees online" | *bit.ly/fEgQHo*

★ PayPal Shortcodes – insert PayPal buttons in your posts or pages using a shortcode | *bit.ly/eUjhgM*

★ View a complete list of WordPress e-commerce plugins | *bit.ly/eTEkwZ*

Many e-commerce platform sites come with an in-built payment system. Here are the main ones.

PayPal

Regarded as the leading international payment platform, PayPal has more than 84 million active registered accounts and is available in 190 markets, meaning you can successfully trade in all these markets!

For online store owners, PayPal is easy to introduce and offers customers peace of mind that payment will be secure. Indeed, PayPal's total payment volume in 2009 represented nearly 15% of global e-commerce.

The company offers three main products: website payments standard, website payments pro and express checkout. To enable your customers to buy multiple items, use a free PayPal shopping cart. To put the 'Add to Cart' button on your website with HTML code you can simply copy and paste from PayPal to the coding of your own site. Your customers then click the button to make a purchase.

★ Add PayPal button | *bit.ly/blxrUn*

With PayPal, there are no set-up charges, monthly fees or cancellation charges, and fee levels vary depending on the volume of sales.

★ *www.paypal.co.uk*

Google Checkout

Google Checkout is a global payment system. There are no set-up charges and fees depend on the volume of your sales. With monthly sales of less than £1,500, the fee is currently 3.4% plus £0.20 per transaction. This transaction fee decreases in line with sales volumes increasing.

★ *checkout.google.co.uk*

Sage Pay

Sage Pay is a card payment service that allows you to accept payments by PayPal and major debit and credit cards. It is simple to manage and easy to integrate within your website. The fee is £20 per month for merchants processing up to 1,000 transactions per quarter and 10p per transaction for merchants processing more than 1,000 transactions per quarter, with a minimum charge of £20 per month. There are no set-up fees, no percentage fees and no annual charges.

★ *www.sagepay.com*

TIP: Just-in-time payment

Adding a PayPal payment button to your site will enable you to accept payment from all major credit and debit cards, as well as bank accounts around the world. You can set it up in less than 15 minutes.

For more information on e-commerce, view the video series '10 steps to e-commerce success' produced by Enterprise Nation in association with PayPal: *bit.ly/gEdpWO*

Distance Selling Regulations

One thing to bear in mind when selling goods or services to consumers via the internet, mail order or by phone, is compliance with the Consumer Protection (Distance Selling) Regulations 2000. The key features of the regulations are:

* You must offer consumers clear information including details of the goods or services offered, delivery arrangements and payment, the supplier's details and the consumer's cancellation right before they buy (known as prior information). This information should be provided in writing.

There are some important regulations to comply with when selling online

* The consumer has a period of seven working days from delivery of the items to cancel their contract with you.

* These regulations only apply when selling to consumers, as opposed to businesses. In the event of a contract being ceased, you have to refund money, including delivery charges, within 30 days of the date of cancellation.

For more guidance, see: *tinyurl.com/63798kq*

Keep customers coming back with offers and good service and attract new customers by making some noise and rising up the search engine ranks!

Top 12 sales tips for the craft industry

Jackie Wade, MD of Winning Sales and author of *Successful Selling for Small Business* gives her top 12 tips for face-to-face sales success:

Think of selling in the positive and good old-fashioned context of 'sales assistant'. You don't have to be pushy, aggressive or in-your-face to be successful at selling. You need to focus instead on helping or *assisting* your customers to buy well and hopefully that means buy you.

Seek to engage with your potential customers. Smile, be warm and friendly and above all be natural. Be you.

Don't be aloof or put physical barriers in the way. If you're selling on a stall or at an exhibition or standing behind a table or counter, come around and stand next to your customer. Seek to connect through your body language and eye contact.

Talk to your customers – don't sell at them. Ask them simple things like "How are you enjoying the fair?", "Have you made any interesting purchases so far?" Build rapport, than seek to chat about their specific needs in relation to your product – who's it for, what's the occasion, when is it … "How can I help you today?"

Equally **be careful about talking too much** or trying to tell them too much about your product. Tell them what they need to know and focus on the key benefits and USPs (unique selling points, i.e. what makes your product or you different).

Listen to your potential customers. Ask them about their needs and wants before offering the product *you* think is right. Don't try and sell until you understand them and their situation and then seek to match the right product to the right customer.

Seek feedback – don't be afraid to ask "What do you think?", "How does that feel for you?", "Is this the kind of thing you're looking for?". You need to be getting positive feedback if you are going to close successfully and get the sale.

If you are receiving positive feedback or noticing positive body language or *buying signals* (nods, gestures, smile), don't forget to ask for the business. "So would you be happy to take one and try it out?", "Would you like me to book in an appointment to come and look at your house and we can discuss colour…?" Sometimes people need a little gentle nudge to take action. This is not the same as being pushy – it's encouragement.

Don't feel under pressure to drop your price or barter. If people say something seems a little dear, ask "I'd be interested to know why you feel that/think that?" Explain the value of what you do and be confident about your price. Offer extras if you must but avoid discounting as it devalues you and your product. Remember, it's not a car boot sale!

Don't forget Added Value Sales. Can you cross-sell and sell two or three items instead of one? Try not to be shy, people are often happy to know that one thing goes nicely with something else. "We have lovely cushions to match those rugs" or "This necklace would really work well with that top". Don't forget, people can always say no and remember even then, it's not personal. Generally, people like to receive good and genuine advice and tips. Be proactive, don't wait to be asked.

Remember in the craft industry, YOU are an important part of your product so make sure you share with customers your expertise, uniqueness and history, if it helps to add value to the product or purchase. Again don't be afraid to blow your own trumpet in the nicest possible way. No one else will. And remember – look the part.

And finally, **always be thinking about future sales**. If someone buys today, let them know where and how they can buy again. Ask them to recommend or introduce other people they know to you and your product. They will happily do that if they like you. If they don't buy today, how can they reconnect with you when they are ready or when they change their mind? Make it easy for people to find and buy from you. It will greatly increase the return you get from your investment to participate at a trade-fair, show or market.

Jackie Wade is MD of Winning Sales and author of Successful Selling for Small Business
www.brightwordpublishing.com/successfulselling

Chapter Seven

Make some noise!

S ales are coming in and you want to tell the world about you and your new business. Profile brings new customers, new sales and headlines!

GETTING KNOWN

Become known in the press and online by making friends with the media, hosting events, entering awards and becoming an expert in your field. Create the right first impression, whether a customer meets you at an event or visits you online. Here's guidance on how to achieve it all. First step: getting known.

Boosting your profile is essential – and can be done with some simple steps

Plot the script

Imagine yourself as the star of your own Hollywood movie. Are you an action hero, battling against the odds (think James Dyson) or a brand-leading lady (think Nigella Lawson)? Plot the action and write the script. It will help you define your message to the media.

Find the right contacts

Research the journalists you think are interested in your field. Note their email addresses from the bottom of their articles, follow them on Twitter, get to know them and send them exclusive stories about you and your business.

TIP: Following the media

Follow media contacts and channels on Twitter to pick up on profile opportunities. Here are a few from radio/TV/magazines:

- ★ @BBCBreakfast

- ★ @BBCOnTheMoney

- ★ @talktothepress

- ★ @findaTVexpert

- ★ @TheTimesLive

- ★ @guardian

- ★ @countrylivingUK

- ★ @real_business

- ★ @bizmattersmag

Please contact Enterprise Nation with your story as we are always profiling start-ups and small businesses on our website, in books (like this one!), in kits, in videos and as part of the national StartUp Britain campaign.

Submit your story at *www.enterprisenation.com*.

Write a release

Writing a press release costs nothing but your time, yet it can generate thousands of pounds worth of publicity. If you're emailing a press release to journalists, write the text in the body of the email and include it in an attachment, too.

Your press release should have an attention-grabbing headline, the main facts in the first sentence and evidence and quotes from as high-profile people and companies as possible in the main body of the text. Include great quality images wherever you can to lift the piece and put a face to the brand (but don't make the email file size huge!). You could also use a press-release distribution service to secure wider exposure. My personal favourite is Response Source (*www.responsesource.com*) but there's also PR Newswire (*www.prnewswire.co.uk*) and PRWeb (*www.prweb.com*). If you don't get a response, follow up!

Just In Time PR

A new service from Rhizome PR has been launched with a promise of 'no coverage, no fee' – register with the site, be contacted when a quote is required from someone with your skills and expertise and only pay when your quote is used!

★ *www.justintimepr.com*

TIP: Link request

If you're being featured online ask the journalist if they can include a live link to your site. That way, readers can be on your site within a click.

PR is the perfect kick-start!

Greg Simpson, founder and director of Press for Attention gives his top eleven tips for building a successful PR campaign:

1. Have a 'cunning plan'

Too many people rush into PR and marketing campaigns with no real plan.

* What are the goals of the campaign?

* How do you want to come across in terms of tone?

* Key messages – what do you want to get across?

* Strategy – consider how various companies get their messages across.

* Tactics – PR stunts, press releases, controversy, photo opportunities, comment/opinion pieces, debates, flash mobs, press trips, celebrity endorsements, competitions.

There are so many ways to get noticed. Blend them to your requirements and skills.

2. Research your customer/audience

There is little point getting a full article page in *Dog Grooming Monthly* if you sell organic ice-cream to boutique hotels! Find out who your ideal customer is and research what they read, listen to and watch. Then, REALLY take the time to read the publications and get to know what sort of stories they publish.

3. Find the news hook

Be honest, is your story really news?

Examples include: new products, new staff, new promotions, new premises, anniversaries, company expansion, financial milestones and charity efforts.

You can also provide topical comment on a newsworthy subject. Keep an eye out for issues that affect your business or your customers. This takes practice and you need to establish credibility in your subject area first. Consider starting a blog that provides regular, lively and informed comment in your area of expertise to build your profile. I use Wordpress which is free.

4. Got a story?

Great! Now you need a SIMPLE press release for a journalist to refer to. People worry that their efforts don't sound flashy enough to warrant attention but you aren't aiming for a Booker Prize, you are aiming for coherent and interesting NEWS.

Use "Who, What, When, How and Why?" as a framework and imagine yourself as the journalist. Is this definitely of interest to their readers? Is it simple enough to understand? Does it stand up on its own?

I would stick to a maximum of 300 words and keep the press release focused on the news angle.

5. Hit them between the eyes

Journalists get hundreds of press releases every day. Ensure that the headline and first paragraph sum up the entire story in a nutshell. Ideally, your press release should still make sense even if an editor dropped two or three paragraphs.

I call the journalist beforehand to outline my story. This helps iron out any creases and demonstrates that you are trying to work with them and their audience.

6. Don't be tempted to start hassling

I very rarely chase a journalist once I have sent a press release. If it is good enough, they will use it. Hassling will not push it to the top of the pile and may see it heading towards the recycle bin. Be patient and able to help if the journalist does come back and don't go on holiday the day after you have sent a story out!

7. Photos – think in pictures

Consider what makes you read a story when you flick through a newspaper. Headlines play their part but the impact of an interesting picture is greater still. People "sell" stories, so ensure that anyone in your shot is clearly visible and captioned. Try to show the impact of the news – product shots are ok but a product in the hands of a customer is better.

8. Build a relationship

PR is not a 'them vs. us' war with journalists, it is a working relationship where both parties stand to gain. They get news/insight and you get free publicity in exchange for a fresh take on things or for your role in illustrating the impact of an issue with greater clarity.

9. Measure and evaluate

How do you know if your gym regime and new diet is working? You get on the scales (peeking from between your fingers). Are you getting through to the right journalists? How many stories are you sending out? How many are getting coverage? How much coverage do they get? Do your pictures and even your key messages get included? Are you being invited to comment on topical issues?

10. Put your PR hat on and execute the plan

I know many small businesses that freeze when it comes to actually putting their plans into action. Schedule and commit to some time every week to do something that contributes to your PR campaign.

11. A final tip

PR agencies spend vast amounts on media monitoring software for mentions of their clients or to keep in touch with specific debates. You can do a lot of it for free. Have a play with Google Alerts.

Further tips can be found on Greg's website www.pressforattention.com.

Greg Simpson is the founder and director of Press For Attention PR. He began his career as a journalist and has worked in PR for over a decade, representing firms that vary from international PLCs to charities, not-for-profits and start-up businesses.

TIP: An image speaks louder than words

When a picture speaks a thousand words you can afford to talk less! Consider hiring a professional photographer to take pictures of you and your work. Maybe you can do this as a barter deal? Pick up your own digital camera and do it yourself or contact your local college and ask if any photography students would like to offer their time so you receive a free image and the student has material for their portfolio. A journalist is much more likely to cover your story if you have great imagery to go with it. Use the images on your website and in promotion materials and let your business speak for itself.

Talent into turnover

NAME: LISE BECH
TALENT: BASKETMAKING
BUSINESS: BECH BASKETS

Lise's first encounters with basketmaking, while training as an occupational therapist after moving to England from her native Denmark, were far from promising. "Making cane structures with the patients didn't do anything for me at all," she remembers. A decade later, however, while working on a Community Peace Project for the Quakers in Northern Ireland, she discovered how working with willow could give the craft a whole new dimension.

> "I did a course there with Alison Fitzgerald, who also grew her own crop. I loved the process of weaving with it and was really drawn towards the idea of a material I could grow and harvest myself. I very much wanted to be part of the whole cycle of making something."

When Lise moved to Scotland in the mid 1980s, she was determined to pursue her newfound hobby while living as self-sufficiently and sustainably as possible. Alison gave her 100 willow cuttings to plant on the bare acre of land that surrounded the then-rundown cottage.

"I created a willow bed in our first year here and then began harvesting ten months later. From that point, willow has really ruled my life," Lise says. Today, she has about 800 plants interspersed around the woodland she and husband Narada have created to provide shelter and interest.

She grows 22 different varieties providing her with a wide palette of colours for her weaving, from silvery greys, vivid greens and oranges to deep blues, purples and an intense black. "I usually work with unstripped willow to allow the hues and changing tones of the bark to form an intrinsic element of the finished product," she explains. "Every basket is a one-off – they're not manufactured to uniform standards."

In the early days Lise was simply driven by a desire to master the basics: "At that time the only books available were about weaving with cane, not willow. All I had was one leaflet about how to make a log basket and, using a great deal of trial and error, I tried to adapt this method to different designs. I knew that I needed more tuition if I was going to succeed but willow basketmaking had virtually died out in Scotland."

So she made contact with an English basketmaker, Colin Manthorpe, who had learnt his trade as an apprentice in the 1950s, and arranged for him to come to Scotland and teach courses for herself and a few others. "He showed us all the traditional skills and then I spent hours practising – eventually my round baskets were round and my square ones square."

Wanting to encourage others to discover the joys of willow weaving and fearing that basketmaking in Scotland faced complete extinction, Lise became an early member of the Scottish Basketmakers' Circle (SBC). To spread the word, she has travelled all over Scotland, teaching courses and taking willow cuttings wherever she went to encourage others to grow their own. The SBC now has 150 members with 20 of these making a living from the craft.

Over the years Lise has managed to merge the roles of grower, designer, maker, marketer and teacher into one, with her work selling at prestigious fairs and galleries across the country, but she's never happier than when she's weaving in the workshop. "I may be feeling worried or tense but the rhythm of the weaving has a meditative effect that relaxes me," Lise says. "It allows me to express myself but it's more than my work and my hobby – it's therapy. And what other artwork smells so good?"

Top tip

"Get your work photographed by a professional who has been recommended by other makers and has experience/love of craftwork. Look at his/her portfolio and be present during the shoot. Good digital photographs (on a white background) will get your work seen by many more people than will see the actual piece! Use them on your website, business cards, swingtickets, press releases, exhibition applications. etc. A portrait of you at work is also useful to have!"

★ *www.bechbaskets.net*

ENTER AWARDS

Enter awards and competitions and enjoy the press coverage that goes with it. Many award schemes are free to enter and are targeted at young start-up businesses. Writing the entry will help to clarify your goals and vision, and winning will bring profile and prizes.

Talent into turnover

NAME: SUE POWELL
TALENT: BAKING
BUSINESS: THE GLUTEN FREE KITCHEN

Sue Powell's business, The Gluten Free Kitchen Ltd., had humble beginnings in her North Yorkshire home seven years ago but has since gone on to supply the likes of the National Trust, Booths supermarket chain in the North West, Buckingham Palace garden parties, Budgens supermarkets, five wholesale distributors including one in Eire, as well as a thriving 'online' shop.

Sue, a former Metropolitan Police officer, wasn't really looking to start a business when she first got involved with gluten-free baking. Six years before the business began to take shape, she had moved to North Yorkshire and ran a country pub before training as a chef. A short while later her friend needed some help manning her coffee shop during a particularly busy Bank Holiday and Sue offered to help.

"I waited tables at a tea room in Aysgarth, which had a reputation for serving specialist foods," Sue says. "I was astounded by the demand for gluten-free soups. People would come from 50 miles away just so they could sit in a normal environment and enjoy a meal."

As a result, Sue began to look more into coeliac disease and what sufferers can and can't eat. When Sue asked Karen's coeliac customers what they missed, their cravings for home-cooked comfort foods struck a chord.

"I've always loved making sweet things. When I ran the pub, my bread-and-butter pudding was a bestseller," she says. "I saw a need for fresh, traditional baking, so I bought some gluten-free ingredients and started messing around in my kitchen. The first thing I attempted was Bakewell tart – you could have built a house with my first batch of pastry!"

Several weeks and many discarded recipes later, Sue perfected her crust using a blend of potato, rice, maize and sarrasin (buckwheat) flours. The tart was an instant hit at the tea rooms and soon Sue added rhubarb crumble and other feel-good puddings to her repertoire. When word spread and demand became overwhelming, Sue gave up her job in a local restaurant kitchen and went into cake-making full time. "My husband, Dave, and I put our heads together and decided to go for it. But we were determined to do it properly."

They have won many awards since starting baking and are proud of winning first prize in the Foods Matter FreeFrom Food Awards gluten free cake section in 2008, 2009, and 2010, with three different cakes. This meant evicting Dave from his home office and, with the help of start-up grants and a considerable amount of their savings, converting it into a purpose-built kitchen.

"Keeping the business separate from our home kitchen is essential to avoid contamination," says Sue, who also produces wheat-free, dairy-free and egg-free products for people with different allergies. "The whole purpose of what I am doing is to give people the pleasure of eating food that they know is safe."

The Gluten Free Kitchen is now in it's fourth premises, employing five full and part-time staff with plans to take on more people in the near future. This might enable Sue to work fewer 16-hour days and spend more time riding her horse and relaxing with her two spaniels at home. "Interest in our business and the 'free from' market in general is booming. I have seen a tremendous growth in awareness and interest in the last 12 months." They currently have interest from one of the large multiples and have a company looking to export their products to Germany and other locations in Europe.

As for the long term, Sue's ambitions are modest. "It's important to me to remain hands-on in the kitchen. Ideally, I'd like to have a dozen people working for me – a small, happy, busy business."

Top tip

"Limit your range to a manageable level, and don't take on too much, too soon."

★ *www.glutenfreefood.info*

To find out about upcoming awards, visit *www.awardsintelligence.co.uk* or check out the following:

★ *Country Living* Magazine Kitchen Table Talent Awards – if you're working on a talent or skill from the kitchen table and know it can be turned into a business, this competition is for you. Prizes include office equipment, profile in the magazine and advice/support from business experts! | *www.allaboutyou.com/countryliving*

★ Shell LiveWIRE Grand Ideas Awards – up to six awards per month of £1,000 for anyone aged 16 to 30 looking to get an idea off the ground. | *www.shell-livewire.org/awards*

★ The Pitch 2011 – enter regional heats and pitch to experienced judges for a place in the national finals. Takes place across the UK. | *www.thepitch2011.com*

★ Social Enterprise Awards – celebrates social enterprises of all ages. | *www.socialenterprise.org.uk/pages/social-enterprise-awards.html*

- ★ Nectar Small Business Awards – offers cash prizes and plenty of Nectar points! | *www.nectar.com/business-sba2011*

- ★ Startups Awards – celebrating small businesses of all shapes and sizes. | *www.startupsawards.co.uk*

Alex Gooch has won an array of impressive awards which offer credibility to his business and a boost to sales …

Talent into turnover

NAME: ALEX GOOCH
TALENT: BAKER
BUSINESS: ALEX GOOCH BREAD

It was whilst working as head chef at Penrhos Court hotel in Herefordshire when Alex Gooch developed a love of bread.

"The hotel owner, Daphne Lambert, is an incredible breadmaker and she encouraged and supported me. She showed a lot of patience as the kitchen looked more like a bakery than a restaurant a lot of the time!"

When Alex could no longer resist the temptation to start his own bread-making business, Daphne allowed him to use one of the hotel kitchens to work through the night baking for local farmers markets and food festivals.

"The response was massive so after a few months of markets I started sorting out funding and looking for premises. September 2007 was when I started baking from Daphne's kitchen and in August 2008 I opened my bakery in Hay-on-Wye."

Alex secured free business training from the welsh assembly government and a £5000 grant which, combined with financial help from his brother and a loan from Finance Wales provided the funding to get up and running.

Little of this money had to be spent on marketing and promotion as Alex's business has grown through word of mouth recommendations. Winning awards has also increased sales with Alex winning the overall festival loaf competition at Ludlow food festival in 2008, Food Producer of the Year in the Waitrose and *Country Living* Made in Britain awards in 2009 and Best Food Producer in the BBC Radio 4 Food &Farming awards in 2010. That's quite a stack of trophies!

"My bread is about traditional processes based on long fermentation and using what I believe to be the best ingredients. A lot of my ingredients are very local; my organic eggs are from down the road, my garlic is grown a couple of miles away, I get soft fruit from my father-in-law and apples from my Dad. High-quality ingredients are a big part of my bread, whether it's organic butter from a Welsh cooperative farm (Calon Wen) or organic single variety extra virgin olive oil from Calabria in Italy."

Having received many requests for courses, Alex is responding to market demand and growing the business by introducing bread courses and mail-order bread. He's developing these avenues with help from food experts such as Mark Glynne-Jones of Jump To! creative agency and a big dollop of support from his family.

"My Dad has worked in the business from the start. He is very popular at the markets!"

It's not only Alex's Dad who's popular at markets; that bread is making quite an impression too!

Top tip

"Believe in yourself. If you have the passion and drive and are prepared to work hard anything is possible. For the first 18 months of my business I did 90-100 hour weeks, most of the time with a smile on my face because I loved what I was doing. Bread for me is an obsession, and I think your heart has to be in a new business 100% to make it work."

★ Watch Alex in action | *www.crisbarnett.com/video-home/organic-baker*

See page 258 for details of the Food Funnel developed by Jump To! to help artisan and food-based businesses rapidly access markets and scale in size.

HOST AN EVENT

Invite the press to come and meet you. This doesn't have to be an expensive affair; the secret is partnering with others who would benefit from being in front of your audience. Approach a venue and ask if they would host at no cost in exchange for the venue receiving profile. Do the same with caterers. Then give invited guests a reason to attend – have a theme, an interesting speaker, a launch announcement, something that will grab their attention and encourage them to attend.

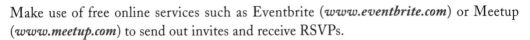

Make use of free online services such as Eventbrite (*www.eventbrite.com*) or Meetup (*www.meetup.com*) to send out invites and receive RSVPs.

TIP: I'm a celebrity. Get me on your product!

One way to attract profile and attention is to have a celebrity endorse your product or service. Lyndsey Young has seen the benefit of this. She is the inventor of Count On It food freshness labels and she secured an endorsement from celebrity mum and actress Amanda Holden, who has used the labels when preparing meals for her daughter. This support has been beneficial in leading to other marketing successes, including features in BBC *Easy Cook*, *Your Homes*, *That's Life*, *Cook Vegetarian* and *Healthy* magazine.

Join a group or club

Signing up to a local business club or network is good for business and your social life. You get together to do deals but also end up making friends. Check out these national business networks to find your natural fit.

* 1230 TWC – events for women in business | *www.1230.co.uk*

* 4Networking – national network of business breakfast groups | *www.4networking.biz*

* The Athena Network – networking organisation for women in business | *www.theathenanetwork.com*

* Business Scene – hosts regional and national networking events as well as hosting an online directory of over 10,000 events across the UK | *www.business-scene.com*

* Ecademy – national site with local and regional meet-ups | *www.ecademy.com*

* Jelly – an American import which encourages casual gatherings of co-workers, with events held in people's homes, the local coffee shop or workspaces. The idea is that you meet in relaxed surroundings and creative ideas are stimulated by the experience. There are now Jelly events taking place in all corners of the UK. | *www.uk-jelly.org.uk*

* School for Startups – headed by serial entrepreneur Doug Richard, School for Startups travels the UK hosting events for anyone considering starting a business. Gems from Doug's presentations are broadcast via S4STV. | *www.schoolforstartups.co.uk*

* Women in Rural Enterprise (WiRE) – networking and business club for rural women in business | *www.wireuk.org*

* First Friday – a free business networking event held monthly; informal gatherings in a welcoming environment | *www.firstfriday-network.co.uk*

* StartUp Saturday – a weekly class hosted by Enterprise Nation that not only offers instruction on how to start a business but also ensures a ready-made support group for anyone wishing to become their own boss. | *www.startupsaturday.co.uk*

There are also chambers, associations, trade groups and enterprise agencies who host regular events:

* British Chambers of Commerce | *www.britishchambers.org.uk*

* Federation of Small Businesses (FSB) | *www.fsb.org.uk*

* Forum of Private Business | *www.fpb.org*

* National Enterprise Network | *www.nationalenterprisenetwork.org*

* Professional Contractors Group (PCG) | *www.pcg.org.uk*

National bodies that hold events and offer support at certain stages in your entrepreneurial career include:

NACUE – standing for The National Consortium of University Entrepreneurs, this is a national organisation that represents university-based enterprise societies across the UK and hosts events to encourage student entrepreneurship.

* *www.nacue.com*

National Centre for Entrepreneurship in Education (NCEE) – a body responsible for raising the profile of entrepreneurship in education across the FE and HE sectors, stimulating cultural change in institutions to create environments in which entrepreneurial aspiration and endeavour can flourish and encouraging and supporting the option of starting a business or a new venture as a future life choice amongst students, graduates and staff.

★ *www.ncee.org.uk*

PRIME (The Prince's Initiative for Mature Enterprise) – a network for the over 50s that provides free information, events and training. PRIME also offers loans through an innovative scheme with online lender Zopa and the charitable arm of Bank of America.

★ *www.prime.org.uk*

★ *www.primebusinessclub.co.uk*

From attending events you may meet businesses with whom there is a shared opportunity. *See page 248 onwards for details on how to draw up a basic partnership agreement.*

Start with StartUp Britain

Visit the StartUp Britain website which offers links to events, awards, activities and other useful resources for start-ups and growing businesses: *www.startupbritain.org*

StartUp Britain offers lots of support and resources

ATTEND TRADE SHOWS

Promote your brand by attending the shows your customers attend. Craft fairs and shows are excellent places to sell products, meet customers and get your business in front of the ideal target audience. See the next page for trade show and fairs tips and techniques!

Shows and fairs: the perfect sales and marketing opportunity

Start by deciding on the type of craft fair you want to exhibit at, i.e. where your customers are likely to be. Then look at location – is the fair out of town, meaning hotel and transport costs and, if so, are there ways you could reduce your expenditure, for example staying with friends, or sharing costs with another business?

Carry out online searches and talk to other crafters to find out the best fairs to attend and keep updated with crafting blogs and websites for mention of the more popular events. Don't forget your local shops and newsletters/magazines as these are often a source of useful information.

Confident you've found the right fair, look at how much exhibition space you'll need and can afford. Look carefully at what is included in the exhibition price/space – will they provide a table and chairs, electricity, an internet connection? Most events will have an online or paper application process; be clear about what you do, make and sell – the organisers may have thousands of people applying for space so make their decision as easy as possible. Once happy with your application form, press send and wait! It may take a couple of days before you receive confirmation.

You've been accepted!

If you have been accepted for the fair, congratulations!

There will be lots to do to get you ready to exhibit so some key points to start with:

* **Make a list of what you have in stock** – do you have enough of each product to take with you, or will you need to produce some extra stock? How will you price these items, and will you be displaying prices on them, or will you have a clear price list which people can refer to?

* **Your exhibition space will need to be decorated** – think about sourcing items and backdrops that will highlight your brand and your message, and show off products to their best advantage. For example, do you sell handmade rings? Instead of having them laid flat in a box, could you display them on a hand mannequin or use a prop to dangle them from? If you sell clothing, do you need to take a mirror? These little things can make the difference between someone buying your product or walking away. Think about stalls you have visited when you've been at craft fairs and the ones that stood out to you – can you take inspiration from them to create your own stand?

* **Don't forget marketing materials,** such as business cards, flyers and special offer leaflets. Do you have these ready or will you need to produce them? Do you have anything you can use as a handout to passers-by?

* **Packaging materials** – you will need to ensure you have enough of this to last you for the entire fair. If you wrap your products up, it could be a nice idea to invest in some stickers with your logo and website details to seal the package, so that when the customer gets home they remember you and your stall and may be tempted to buy again. You could even look at customised carrier bags – extra advertising as your customers wander around the fair.

* Ahead of the event, ask organisers how the **drop-off and delivery process** works so you have enough time to set up your stall and get yourself ready before customers begin to arrive and you're out of the venue by the correct time once the event finishes.

* Consider whether you need **public liability insurance** to display your products or, for example, to have public food demonstrations etc.

* Another important point to be considered is how you will take **payment**. Most people will want to pay by cash or credit/debit card so think about how you will offer this.

Talent into turnover

NAME: JO COLWILL
TALENT: QUILTING
BUSINESS: COWSLIP WORKSHOPS

Launceston in Cornwall is the base where Jo Colwill runs Cowslip Workshops, offering a programme of craft classes and attracting textile lovers from all over the globe.

Jo has been quilting for over 30 years but it wasn't until 1996 that Cowslip graduated from occasional gatherings around her antique oak dining table to a full-time business. "I never set out to do it in a big way," Jo explains. "Sewing was simply a hobby that grew. It started off with one class and got busier and busier through word of mouth."

Like many farmers after the foot and mouth crisis of 2001, Jo and her husband Stephen looked at what else they could offer. "We did not look at it as diversification – we were just desperate to stay on the farm. The classes ran for a long while before the foot and mouth but this was the turning point of making a serious business to pay the rent, and then the shop was added. I loved cooking on my 35-year-old, solid fuel Rayburn until it got too much. So then came the café with my dream AGA and the hope of a wind turbine but very much keeping the farmhouse kitchen feel and growing and promoting our own vegetables and meat."

Jo first turned her attention to quilt-making when she married Stephen and they moved into draughty, 400-year old Newhouse Farm, where her husband's family have been tenants since 1907.

"It needed a homely touch," Jo explains. "Farmers never want to spend anything on a house – they'll buy a new tractor but not new curtains, so I made my own. And we needed something cheerful for our bedroom. So I made my first patchwork quilt, just cut-out diamonds of dressmaking fabric stitched over paper. I'm horrified at it now."

She persevered and honed her skills by attending classes and meeting other quilters. Her second effort, a sampler quilt, was borrowed for a magazine shoot by the local home-interiors shop and was immediately snapped up by a customer. Instead of selling it, though, Jo swapped it for a bed. She hasn't looked back.

The workshops, taught by her and by guest tutors, range from basic appliqué to stitching an autumn landscape, rag rugs, willow, painting old furniture, etc. and include contemporary ideas as well as traditional ones. "I love meeting people and you learn as much as you give," says Jo. "People come from London, France, Australia, both young and old. I want them to create something and get a sense of satisfaction."

To that end, she doesn't impose pure quilting on beginners: instead of turning every edge under, she suggests adhesive and a decorative stitch to speed up the process. "I want to encourage people. There is nothing right or wrong in quilting. Every

> *"We love our way of life here. The farm and the workshops support each other."*

person finds a way to express themselves. My aim is that people go home clutching something they have made in a day. One lady has been to so many classes she has made probably 200 cushions!"

The bulk of Jo's creations are class samples, which subsequently sell in the shop. "I do little sketches – on the back of my chequebook sometimes – then do a big drawing to create templates," she says. "I just make it up as I go along. I've got a stash of fabric, including recycled clothes. I find colour and texture exciting and I use a machine to piece the bits together, then do the intricate parts by hand. While I'm working on one little farm quilt, ten more are queuing up in my brain."

She always has a commission on the go as well, though she stresses that the quilting is a collaborative effort from a loose group of friends. "They're all brilliant sewers. Some have learnt here – one did soft-furnishing training, another does costumes at the Theatre Royal in Plymouth. We try to be together in the workroom but they also take a bit home."

Although Jo now employs 15 staff, she mucks in with most tasks. In addition to the stitching and teaching, she stocks the shop and helps out at lambing time. Late at night is when she finally gets time to be alone with her sewing. "I go into the workroom, the dogs settle under the table and I put on some classical music and just sew. I feel frustrated if I'm not creating something."

Cowslip's success bolsters the income from the farm, but it has made inroads on family life, so Jo is keen to involve her husband as much as possible. Hosting community events, such as wassailing evenings and apple days, helps to do that. And the farm location adds interest to outsiders coming for classes: they keep dairy cows, beef cattle and sheep. "People really enjoy seeing the animals," Jo says. "We love our way of life here. The farm and the workshops support each other. One without the other just wouldn't be the same."

Top tip

"Use up those old or unwanted jeans to make a cosy cushion – patchwork started from make do and mend and I like to combine new and old fabrics to give a personal and unique feel to each item and also keep the cost down."

★ *www.cowslipworkshops.co.uk*

Cash

Accepting cash is fairly straightforward. All you'll need to do is set up a small float to provide change and some way of recording sales. The float doesn't have to be enormous – look at the prices you are selling your products for and plan accordingly (round numbers are easiest to deal with). It is a good idea to take along a receipt book so that you can write out receipts for anyone paying cash.

An inventory list will also be invaluable here as this will enable you to keep track of what stock is selling – useful for evaluating sales after the fair and also to keep you on top of what stock is remaining.

Credit/debit cards

Many people nowadays will expect to be able to pay for goods via credit or debit card, so it is a good idea to be able to offer this payment method if you can. After all, you don't want to miss out on sales because you aren't able to take payment.

Accepting card payments is more complicated than accepting cash and it might mean that you have to pay a small fee but it will be beneficial in the long run.

One of the ways you can accept payment is through Worldpay:

WorldPay

WorldPay is one of the UK's leading payment services provider, and as part of their service they offer mobile payment terminals which are ideal for events and trade shows, meaning you can take card payments directly from your stall as long as a GPRS mobile phone signal can be received.

You will need to set up a merchant account, which is a bank account specifically for processing credit and debit card orders. More information on how to do that can be found on the Business Link website – *tinyurl.com/6jhy2yy*

The main benefit of the mobile terminal is that it is flexible, accepting all major credit and debit cards, which is a big plus when selling at events, and you can also arrange a short-term hire – great for an event or trade show. The terminal is also chip and PIN compliant, capable of producing receipts for you to give you to your customer and also an end of day reconciliation report so that you can see all of the transactions throughout the show.

The way the mobile terminal works is as follows:

★ Payment details are entered into the payment device or system and the customer inserts their card into the machine. They will then be prompted to enter their PIN and details of the purchase, details from the card and the PIN are then sent through to WorldPay. They identify the relevant card (Visa, MasterCard, etc.) and send the details through them to the bank that issued the card.

★ The bank then checks the cardholder's identity, that the account has sufficient funds and that the card hasn't been reported lost or stolen. If everything is okay, the issuing bank authorise the amount requested and reserve those funds, completing the payment transaction.

* If the details can't be verified, the payment is normally declined and the shopper or is asked to use another type of payment, exactly as they do in shops, restaurants, etc. It's the same kit.

Your WorldPay merchant account is credited with the value of the card transaction, normally within four working days.

WorldPay will send you a merchant statement which details the transactions processed, and how much you've paid for each transaction.

The cost for the transactions breaks down as follows:

* **Set-up fee:** One-time fee for the set-up of your payment gateway £200.

* **Transaction fees:** For UK debit cards, WorldPay charges 50p per transaction. On other transactions, you pay 4.5% of the value. You will also pay a charge for the hire of the card terminal.

PayPal

PayPal is a safe, fast, secure way to pay for goods online as your financial details are never shared with anyone else, and PayPal safeguards your bank, credit or debit card details.

Creating a PayPal account is quick and easy and won't cost you a thing:
www.paypal.com/uk/signup

Once you have set up an account, you are immediately ready to send and receive money from all over the world.

PayPal recently launched PayPal Mobile, which allows you to send and receive payments via your mobile phone. The new PayPal application is free to download to your iPhone,

Android or BlackBerry and is then ready to go. Once at the fair, all your customers need to do is to log in to their PayPal account and send you the money for their purchases using the email address tied to your PayPal account. Alternatively, if they also have the PayPal app, you can simply bump your phones together to transfer the information using their new software!

More information on Paypal Mobile can be found at:
www.paypal-marketing.co.uk/mobile

Tradeshow top tips

Before the event

* **Negotiate a good deal** – if you're prepared to wait it out, the best deals on stands can be had days before the event is starting. The closer the date, the better the price you'll negotiate as the sales team hurry to get a full house. However, you will need to be fully prepared in terms of stock and your marketing materials.

* **Tell people you're going** – circulate news that you'll be at the event through online networks (giving your location or stand number) and issue a press release if you're doing something newsworthy at the event, maybe launching a new product, having a guest appearance, running a competition, etc.

At the event

* **Be clear on the offer** – determine what you are selling at the show and let this be consistent across show materials; from pop-up stands to flyers. Be creative with the stand to keep costs low. Consider offering a supply of mouth-watering refreshments!

* **Be friendly and approachable** – walk around the stall, talk to people and maybe even wear or hold something that you have made and are selling – this could be a conversation

starter and seeing the product on a person can make a difference. Let people know about the materials you've used or the particular way the product has been made – engage, engage, engage!

* **Pop-ups** – Pop-ups get your business noticed, especially if you're hoping to stand out at an exhibition or a trade show. Staples' Copy & Print Centres can take your design and turn it into a versatile, portable sign in less than an hour.

* **Collect data** – find ways to collect attendees' names and details. Offer a prize in exchange for business cards or take details in exchange for a follow-up information pack or offer. Some events also offer the facility to scan the details from the delegates' badges (for a fee).

* **Take friends/family** – invite a supportive team. If you're busy talking to a potential customer, you'll want others on the stand who can be doing the same. If there's time, get to know the exhibitors around you.

* **Be prepared** – wear comfortable shoes, bring some spare clothes and pack your lunch; if you're busy there may not be time to buy food and drink!

After the event

* **Follow-up** – within a couple of days of returning from the show, contact the people who expressed interest so that interest can be turned into sales.

* **Plan ahead** – if the show delivered a good return, contact the organisers and ask to be considered for a speaking slot or higher profile at the next event, and confirm your willingness to be a case study testimonial story in any post-show promotion.

Craft fairs, useful links and resources

Country Living Spring and Christmas Fairs

★ *www.countrylivingfair.com* | @CLFairs

Events listing via UK Handmade

★ *www.ukhandmade.co.uk/events*

Directory of shops selling handmade goods

★ *www.ukhandmade.co.uk/shopdirectory* | @ukhandmade

Local events

★ *www.ukhandmade.co.uk/localgroups*

★ Suffolk Craft Society | *www.suffolkcraftsociety.org*

★ Glasgow Craft Mafia | *www.glasgowcraftmafia.com*

★ Birmingham Craft Mafia | *www.birminghamcraftmafia.com*

★ Stitch & Craft Show | *www.stitchandcraft.co.uk*

★ Farmers' Markets, national | *www.farmersmarkets.net*

★ London Farmers' Markets | *www.lfm.org.uk*

- ★ British Sellers on Etsy | *britishsellersonetsy.blogspot.com*

- ★ Crafty Fox Pop Up Market | *craftyfoxmarket.blogspot.com*

- ★ Craft Fair Secrets on Folksy | *blog.folksy.com/category/seller-tips/craft-fair-advice*

- ★ Make It, Sell it! event | *www.bl.uk/bipc/workevents/global/friday/makeit.html*

- ★ Art & craft events in Lincolnshire | *www.tempopromotes.co.uk*

- ★ Selvedge Fairs | *www.selvedge.org/pages/fair.aspx*

- ★ Pick 'n' Mix Makers Markets, Norfolk | *picknmixmakersmarket.blogspot.com*

- ★ Craft Guerilla, East London | *www.craftguerrilla.com*

- ★ Crafts Council | *www.craftscouncil.org.uk*

- ★ *Crafts Magazine* | *www.craftscouncil.org.uk/crafts-magazine*

- ★ Hello Etsy | *www.helloetsy.com*

National directory resource for contemporary craft

- ★ *www.craftscouncil.org.uk/craft-directory*

Listing of creative courses

- ★ *www.frombritainwithlove.com/directory/creative-courses*

- ★ Craft Reactor, Edinburgh | *www.craftreactor.com*

We plan to keep building this list – you will find it at *www.enterprisenation.com*. Please add to the list with your own suggestions!

How else can you get your name and products out there in front of people?

BECOME AN EXPERT

Set yourself up as an expert in your field and the media will come knocking on your door. Do this by writing a book, offering training or developing your own app! Here are eight ways in which you can promote your expertise.

1. Publish a book

Become a published author on the topic of your choice by self-publishing via sites such as Lulu, Blurb and Ubyu. Utilise the book as a business development tool, printing on demand to take copies to events, and offering free and downloadable versions to potential customers. Being an author gives you credibility and gives customers information and insight.

* Blurb | *www.blurb.com*

* Lulu | *www.lulu.com*

* Ubyu | *www.ubyubooks.com*

* Brightword Publishing | *www.brightwordpublishing.com*

2. Present yourself

Put yourself forward to speak at events (consider asking for a fee and/or costs to be covered) or suggest being a satellite speaker, where you are beamed into the conference hall via video link-up, so saving the effort and expense of travel. Invite customers and prospects and make the presentation openly available via Slideshare.

* Slideshare | *www.slideshare.com*

3. Host a webinar

Share your expertise or demonstrate a process by hosting a webinar or visual presentation where a 'live' audience can see you and interact. Achieve this via platforms such as GoToMeeting, GoToWebinar, WebEx and Salesforce, and remember to host it at a time that suits your target audience.

* GoToMeeting | *www.gotomeeting.com*

* GoToWebinar | *www.gotowebinar.com*

* WebEx | *www.webex.co.uk*

* Salesforce | *www.salesforce.com*

4. Produce a film

Maybe the word 'film' is a little ambitious but you can create your own video content with an affordable camcorder or smart phone, or by hiring in a cameraman and having a sponsored series of guides that can be uploaded to video sharing sites such as YouTube, Vimeo and eHow, and easily embedded into your site.

* YouTube | *www.youtube.com*

* Vimeo | *www.vimeo.com*

* eHow | *www.ehow.co.uk*

5. Broadcast a podcast

For customers who like to listen to what you have to say at a time that suits them, upload a podcast with top tips, interviews and your thoughts of the day. Make it available on your site, iTunes and Podcast Alley to be sure of a wide audience. Follow advice from podcast producer San Sharma on how to record a podcast on a Skype call.

* Submit a podcast to the iTunes store | *www.apple.com/itunes/podcasts/specs.html*

* Podcast Alley | *www.podcastalley.com*

TIP: How to record a podcast on a Skype call

You can produce a podcast interview using Skype, Pamela Call Recorder, and a little editing know-how. San Sharma shows how it's done, in five simple steps ...

1. Sign up for a free Skype account (*www.skype.com*) and download the Skype software.

2. If you're using a Windows machine, download Pamela Call Recorder (*www.pamela.biz*), which lets you record your Skype calls. If you're on a Mac, you can download Call Recorder for Skype (*www.ecamm.com*). Both have free trial versions, but only cost around £13 when that's expired.

3. Call up your interviewee using Skype. If they're a Skype user, too, that will be a free call but if they're on a fixed or mobile line, you'll need to get some Skype Credit (*bit.ly/epymNm*).

4. Once you've made a connection and agreed with the interviewee the format of the conversation, hit the record button on your call recorder software and you're off!

5. Edit using Audacity (***audacity.sourceforge.net***), which is free for Windows and Macs, or with GarageBand (***www.apple.com/ilife/garageband***), which comes with most Macs (you can also buy it as part of the iLife package).

And the easiest way to share your recording is by uploading it to Audioboo (***www.audioboo.com***), which lets people listen to it on the web, embedded on your website or via iTunes or on a mobile phone.

San Sharma is online community manager at Enterprise Nation (www.enterprisenation.com)

6. Deliver training

Whether your skill is in embroidering handmade shoes or developing stylish websites, your knowledge could be shared with others. Rather than seeing this as surrendering intelligence to potential competitors, offer instruction you're comfortable with that will create fans and followers who will learn from you, buy from you and, critically, encourage others to do the same. Check out platforms GoToTraining and Webtraining, encourage contacts to sign up and then after the demonstration you have a chance to follow up with a group of new contacts.

★ GoToTraining | *www.gototraining.com*

★ WebEx Webtraining | *www.webex.co.uk/products/elearning-and-online-training.html*

7. Develop an app

Take your content and make an iPhone app with browser-based platform AppMakr. It's free to use and you can either set a list price to make sales via the App Store or make it available free of charge.

* AppMakr | *www.appmakr.com*

8. Form groups

Encourage others to discuss, debate and contribute to your content by forming groups utilising social media platforms such as Facebook, LinkedIn and Ning. Bonding interested people to each other will bond them ever closer to you, the content creator and group host.

* Facebook | *www.facebook.com*

* LinkedIn | *www.linkedin.com*

* Ning | *www.ning.com*

TIP: Be everywhere

Keep in touch with existing customers via a newsletter and reach out to the new by making regular appearances at events, on other people's websites and blogs, in newspapers and magazines, and on radio and TV. Write to the magazines and radio stations that ask people to send in their story. It's a free way to get coverage. The more you're covered, the more you'll be invited to speak and comment, and before you know it, you'll be everywhere!

Price point

These publishing options will raise your profile but you can also generate revenue from them. Your options are:

* make your content and knowledge available at no charge to customers, to build your reputation as the go-to person and place for a particular product or service

* charge for access/downloads/viewing and turn your micropublishing activity into a revenue stream in its own right.

Individual judgement will be needed in this and it's something you can assess over time. Start with a mix of charged-for and free content, ensure you are providing good value and incentives for your community to remain engaged, and the options to introduce charged-for content will increase.

ONLINE PROMOTION

Become well known online and attract customers to your site through search engine optimisation, social tagging and pay-per-click advertising.

Rise up the search engine ranks

Search engine optimisation, or SEO, is the process by which you can improve rankings for your website in the top search engines such as Google, so that your site appears on the first few pages of results rather than page 75!

Google uses software known as 'spiders' to crawl the web on a regular basis and find sites to add to its index. There are steps you can take to make it easier for the spiders to find and add your site.

Start with the homepage

Provide high-quality, text-based content on your pages – especially your homepage. If your homepage has useful information and good quality, relevant text, it's more likely to be picked up by the spiders. Beyond the homepage, write pages that clearly describe your topic/service/product. Think about the key words users would type to find your pages and include them on the site.

Make contributions

Identify influential bloggers and sites in your trade/industry, contact them and offer to write posts. You can also improve your visibility by writing helpful comments in forums and on other people's posts.

Be well connected

Improve the rank of your site by increasing the number of other high-quality sites that link to your pages; these are referred to as 'inbound links'. For example, if you're running a competition, go to sites that promote competitions and add yours.

You can also register your site with the major search engines.

* Google | *www.google.co.uk/addurl*
* Yahoo | *search.yahoo.com/info/submit.html*

★ Bing | *www.bing.com/webmaster/submitsitepage.aspx*

TIP: Search engines love links

Another way to increase your ranking in the search results is to link to other sites and vice versa, but think quality here as opposed to quantity. Sites offering the best 'link juice' are trusted domains, such as news sites, and very popular sites. You could post comments on such sites and blogs and include a link back to your site. Also try these handy hints:

★ Approach sites complementary to your own and suggest reciprocal links.

★ Ensure that your website link is included in all your social media profiles.

★ Register with the major search engines (as explained above).

★ Add your domain to local search services and Google Maps (*www.google.co.uk/maps*), Qype (*www.qype.co.uk*), Yahoo! Local (*uk.local.yahoo.com*), BView (*www.bview.co.uk*).

Tagging

A webpage's title, referred to as a 'title tag', is part of the SEO mix and can make a difference to your search rankings. It is also the text that appears in the top of the browser window. Include in your title tag your company name and the main key phrase you'd like the search engines to associate with your webpage, keeping it between 60 and 90 characters in length. Duncan Green of Moo Marketing is an SEO expert and explains:

> "The title tag on the homepage for Moo Marketing reads: 'Moo Marketing – Search Engine Marketing – PPC Management – Search Engine Optimisation'; as you can see, the title element is 85 characters long, contains three key phrases and identifies the subject of the webpage."

Pay-per-click (PPC) advertising

The results from your efforts in SEO will appear on the main engines (Google, Yahoo! and Bing) in the central column of the page as a natural or 'organic' search result. But have you spotted results on the right of the page when searching for items yourself? These are paid-for results and referred to as pay-per-click or PPC advertising. PPC is where you pay to have ads displayed when people type in certain words, in the hope it will attract more visitors to your site.

Google AdWords is such a form of PPC advertising. Think of the key words or phrases you reckon your customers will be searching for and apply them in your Google campaign. Link to your homepage or other pages on the site where you're running a promotion and make the most of geotargeting, which lets you target your ads to specific territories and languages.

You are in full control of the budget and campaign duration.

★ *adwords.google.co.uk*

TIP: Think like a buyer

When thinking of the keywords to use in PPC ad campaigns (and in search engine optimisation) think of the words your buyers will be using when searching for your product or service. Use the Google AdWords Keyword Tool to find out the most popular search terms. Apply these words in the campaign and include them in the text on your site.

Spread the word

Make it easy for visitors to spread word of your site through social sharing. Have your site Stumbled, Dugg and Tweeted and make the most of this viral effect. You can add these social book-marking tools by visiting AddThis (*www.addthis.com*) and choosing the icons you'd like to have displayed on your site.

The most popular are:

* Delicious | *www.delicious.com*

* Digg | *www.digg.com*

* StumbleUpon | *www.stumbleupon.com*

* Twitter | *www.twitter.com*

THE POWER OF SOCIAL MEDIA

5 essential social media tools and how to make the most of them

There have never been so many tools at our disposal that we can use to promote our business free of charge, and without a significant outlay of time. I'm talking about social media. It's time to embrace it.

Embrace social media

According to research company Nielsen, the world now spends over 110 billion minutes on social networks and blogs per month. This equates to 22% of all time online, or one in every four and half minutes.

Embrace this and your business will become known. Here are the five key tools to use and, crucially, how best to use them.

1. **Twitter**

Visit *www.twitter.com*, create an account, start to follow friends and contacts (and their followers) and get tweeting. Follow Mark Shaw's steps for Twitter success.

Cost: free

10 top tips to Twitter success

Mark Shaw, author of *Twitter Your Business* and award-winning ex sales guy that advises and trains people how to use Twitter to gain more business and to be effective with their time provides his 10 top tips that will have you using Twitter far more effectively.

1. **Why be on Twitter?** – This is the first question you need to ask yourself. Think about all the possible reasons you may want to utilise Twitter as this will help you to build a useful strategy and give you an indication on possible resources that you will need.

2. **Who will be tweeting?** – Nothing happens on Twitter just by having an account. It needs someone behind it who understands Twitter and enjoys using it. This is not a technical job. The best person to take this role is usually the business owner. They are the ones that are most passionate about their business, fully understand it and can't stop talking about it.

3. **What is success?** Before you start using Twitter it is important that you think about what success would look like for you. You can then put into place ways to measure those things. It may be simply more website traffic, more sales, more sign ups for your newsletter. All these things can be easily measured.

4. **Be committed** – Add a good photo, perhaps a bespoke background, your website URL and an interesting bio. Your bio is only 160 characters so make sure you use all of them. Try and differentiate yourself and make sure it contains keywords so that others can find you.

5. **Be consistent** – Show up each day and tweet even if you don't have much time. It's more important to do a small amount each day than lots on one day and then nothing for a week or so.

6. **Be interesting** – Try and tweet 3 types of messages: social chit-chat; the sharing of resources, links, tools, info, ideas and opinions; and tweets that answer questions which demonstrate your knowledge. Aim for a good balance, that's the key.

7. **Be interested** – Engage with others by answering questions and joining in. Find conversations to enter into via *www.twitter.com/search* and retweet (RT) other people's messages if they are of interest to you and your followers. It's not about selling things but it is all about building your brand and credibility.

8. **Don't automate your Twitter activity.** Twitter is all about being personal and building relationships via conversations. You can't do that if you simply broadcast all day long. Twitter is a communication channel not a broadcast station.

9. **Twitter is a marathon and certainly not a sprint.** You don't need to follow thousands within minutes of joining. Start off slowly, follow a few people, start to see how it works, start to send out a few messages and just observe, listen and learn.

10. **Twitter is a social platform.** So have fun and be sociable. Twitter should not be a chore. It should be something that you enjoy taking part in. Twitter is not a substitute for other marketing activities but a bolt on to other things.

You can follow Mark at @markshaw. Buy Mark's eBook Twitter your Business *at*
www.brightwordpublishing.com/twitter

2. Facebook

Facebook is the most popular social networking site in the world. The site has over 500 million users worldwide, so if you need to be where your customers are, there's a good chance some of them will be there!

You can list on Facebook for free and/or advertise on the site and select an audience based on location, age and interest. As an advertiser you control how much you want to spend and set a daily budget. The minimum budget is US $1.00 (63p) a day. After designing your ad(s), decide how long you want the campaign to run and whether you want to be charged for the number of clicks you receive (CPC – charge per click) or the number of times your ad is displayed. Visit *www.facebook.com*, create an account, invite friends and contacts to join your group and get promoting.

Listing cost: free

3. LinkedIn

Referring to itself as "the world's largest professional network", LinkedIn has 75 million members in over 200 countries. Visit *www.linkedin.com*, create an account and start connecting with contacts and finding new ones. Form LinkedIn groups around your specialist subject, or, if you are a professional selling creative services, check out the new Creative Portfolio Display application (*linkd.in/deDVX1*), which aims to "empower creative professionals by creating a one-stop solution for maintaining their work portfolio and broadcasting it to millions".

Cost: free (option to upgrade to a business account, which is a paid-for package)

TIP: Top tips from LinkedIn

Present a full picture of yourself

Make sure you add a professional picture so people can easily recognise you and take some time to complete your profile. You'll show up in more search results the more information you provide about your experience and skills. While doing this, picture yourself at a conference or client meeting. How do you introduce yourself? That's your authentic voice and that's what should come across in writing.

Build connections

Connections are one of the most important aspects of your brand – the company you keep reflects the quality of your brand. Identify connections that will add to your credibility and pursue them.

Write a personal tagline

The line of text under your name is the first thing people see in your profile. It follows your name in search hit lists. It's your brand. Ensure it's something that at a glance describes who you are.

Put your elevator pitch to work

Go back to your conference introduction. That 30-second description, the essence of who you are and what you do, is a personal elevator pitch. Use it in the Summary section to engage readers. You've got 5-10 seconds to capture their attention.

Point out your skills

Think of the Specialties field as your personal search engine optimiser, a way to refine the ways people find and remember you. Mention particular abilities and interests, even a note of humour or passion.

Explain your experience

Briefly say what the company does. After you've introduced yourself, describe what you do and what your company does. Use those clear, succinct phrases here.

Distinguish yourself from the crowd

Use the Additional Information section to round out your profile with a few key interests. Maybe you belong to a trade association or an interest group; if you're an award-winner, add prestige by listing that here.

Ask and answer questions

Thoughtful questions and useful answers build your credibility. Make a point of answering questions in your field to establish your expertise and raise your visibility. You may need answers to a question of your own later on.

Recommendations

Pat your own back and others too. Get recommendations from colleagues and clients who will speak credibly about your performance and make meaningful comments when recommending others.

Source: LinkedIn | www.linkedin.com

4. Flickr

Join *www.flickr.com* and promote yourself visually by uploading photos of you and your products or service, and maybe even a few shots of happy customers. The site also carries video clips so you can show:

* events you host, speak at, or attend

* products you make (the finished product) as well as images of the production process

* happy customers wearing/using/enjoying your products and services

* your workspace

* your family (if you – and they – feel comfortable showing your personal side).

You can also easily pull the photos into your blog and social media pages.

Cost: free (option to upgrade to a pro account which is a paid-for package)

ſ. **YouTube**

YouTube is the world's most popular online video community, with 24 hours of video uploaded every minute. Start your own business channel for free, and upload videos profiling you and your work. Create an account (*www.youtube.com/create_account*), start a channel (advice via YouTube video!), and start broadcasting to the world. You can give each of your videos a name and assign keywords to it to help with searching, plus you can have a short description of your company on your profile page. Again, these clips are very easy to add to your website, and they help keep the content fresh and interesting. Footage can even be filmed for free if you have a webcam in your laptop.

Cost: free

Total budget required for online promotion: £0

MEASURE THE RESULTS

Time to measure what's working and what's not. Measure media and press mentions through signing up to Google Alerts – and you'll be pleased to know there's a whole host of tools that are free to use and will show real-time results for what's working on your site and across social media profiles.

Look out, in particular, for the sources of your traffic (which are your highest referring sites) and your most popular pages. You can see days where your site receives spikes in visitor levels (and track this back to marketing) and measure if visitors are spending longer periods on the site and which times are popular, e.g. weekends, evenings, lunchtimes, etc. Google Analytics offers intelligence on your website traffic and marketing effectiveness: *www.google.com/analytics*

There are other analytics options:

* Alexa – web traffic metrics, site demographics and top URL listings | *www.alexa.com*

* Clicky – monitors and analyses your site traffic in real time | *www.getclicky.com*

* Crazy Egg – see which pages visitors are visiting, with a colourful heat map | *www.crazyegg.com*

* Opentracker – gather and analyse web stats and monitor online visitors | *www.opentracker.net*

* StatCounter – an invisible web tracker and hit counter that offers data in real time | *www.statcounter.com*

* Urchin – this is the tool we use to measure and monitor traffic to Enterprise Nation. It is now owned by Google. | *www.urchin.com*

★ Website Grader – generates a free marketing report that compares your site with a competitor's | *www.websitegrader.com*

Hopefully what you will see is an upward curve of visitors and time spent on the site. If you're selling anything then hopefully this means more sales. And if your site is your business, this means you're in a strong position to attract advertisers and begin doing affiliate deals (*see pages 150–1*).

Your website is likely to be the first thing potential customers will see of your business – and they'll make their judgement in seconds! Keep it well polished and visitors will soon become customers.

TIP: A top quality image

Whether you decide to start online with a blog or a full e-commerce offering, use high-quality royalty-free images on your site and printed materials so that on first click or at first glance, a customer is given a good impression and therefore more likely to buy. Take professional images yourself or consider subscribing to a stock image library such as *www.istockphoto.com*. *See page 138 onwards for tips on how to take photos for product display or page 175 for inclusion in press releases.*

Other image libraries include:

★ Image Source | *www.imagesource.com*

★ Photos.com | *www.photos.com*

★ Getty Images | *www.gettyimages.com*

Search for creative commons licensed images you can use commercially from Flickr at *www.compfight.com*.

Chapter Eight

Putting on a professional face

FIRST IMPRESSIONS COUNT

Your marketing activity is going to plan and the business is attracting interest and enquiries from potential customers. Greet them in a professional way and make that first impression count.

Look at my logo!

Customers will get an immediate sense of your style from your logo and company branding. Impress with a nice-looking company design that's repeated across promotional materials, from business cards to brochures.

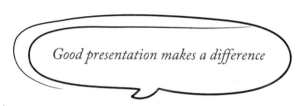

Good presentation makes a difference

Think about what you'd like as your company font, colours and layout. Have a go at designing this yourself or hire the services of a designer/neighbour/friend. Good presentation can make a world of difference. And it may just be the difference you need to clinch a contract.

Find a professional to design your logo via these sites:

* Crowdspring | *www.crowdspring.com*

* 99 designs | *www.99designs.com*

* Enterprise Nation | *www.enterprisenation.com*

* Concept Cupboard | *www.conceptcupboard.com*

* BuildaBrand | *www.buildabrand.com*

Office address

If you are running your business from home there are a couple of reasons why you might not want to put the address on your business card: it might sound too domestic, and you might not want people turning up on your doorstep!

You can solve this with a P.O. Box number, which starts at £170 per year and is easily set up with Royal Mail (*www.royalmail.com/pobox*). Alternatively, you could invest in a virtual office, which gives you a more tailored and personal service than a P.O. Box – plus you get a nice-sounding address and a place to meet other home business owners and clients. Having a virtual office enables you to choose the address that suits you best, have post delivered to that location, and then forwarded on to you. Companies providing this service include:

* Regus | *www.regus.com*
* Mail Boxes Etc. | *www.mbe.co.uk*
* eOffice | *www.eoffice.net*

When holding meetings, consider hiring professional meeting space. Many offer serviced addresses and secretarial services too, so there could be great continuity for your clients if they only have to remember one location.

Make the most of the email marketing opportunity every time you click 'send'. Include a professional email signature or sign-off that has your basic contact details (name, company, postal address, telephone, etc.) and also maybe mention any seasonal or product offers. Indeed, you are required by law, following the introduction of the Companies Act 2006, to display the company's registered office address on your website and any electronic communications.

On the phone

When running a business from home, consider who will be picking up the phone! It's cheap and sometimes free to get an 0845 local rate number or an 0870 national rate number for your business. This will hide where you're based and divert your calls to wherever you specify. But beware: sometimes having such a number – especially with national rates – might put customers off ringing you.

If you use a landline number it's best to have a separate line for your home and your business. It will stop your business calls from being answered by the kids and also give you a chance to escape work calls when you want to. And these days you don't need to invest in an actual second line. I use a VoIP (voice over internet protocol) phone, which uses my broadband internet connection to make and receive calls, something we looked at earlier (*page 70*).

* Skype | *www.skype.com*

Another idea is to get some help from a call-handling service. They will answer your calls with your company name, text urgent messages to you and email the others, giving you a big business feel for about £50 per month. We use a service called Moneypenny, but there are other providers too, including Regus and Answer.

* Moneypenny | *www.moneypenny.biz*

* Regus | *www.regus.co.uk*

* Answer | *www.answer.co.uk*

You might consider a 'follow-me number' to ensure you're available when you need to be and able to deliver the right impression to clients. This involves choosing a number and directing calls from it to your landline or mobile. The beauty is that you have the option to select either a freephone or a geographical number so, say you'd like to have a Manchester area code, simply buy a number starting with 0161. The same goes for hundreds of other locations.

Route calls to your mobile and choose a local number in any of 21 countries to have a virtual local presence with Skype (*www.skype.com*). Offer virtual phone numbers where the caller pays a local rate, regardless of where you are, through Vonage (*www.vonage.co.uk*) or direct calls to you from a chosen number using internet technology and a virtual receptionist at eReceptionist (*www.ereceptionist.co.uk*).

In print

Print is far from dead, so get yourself some business cards, postcards and promotional flyers to hand out at business events, social occasions, and to just about anyone you meet! Have fun with designing your materials and include images relating to your trade. Sell vintage fashion? Include pictures of your products. Offer web design services? Have a portfolio of sites you've designed nicely displayed.

Business cards

It used to be a bit of a palaver to get business cards printed, as well as expensive. First there was a designer to brief, you had to order a thousand at a time and they often took weeks to arrive. These days you can pop into most stationers, tell them what you want and they can print a set in minutes, while you wait – or you can come back later to collect. Or order online via the links below.

* ★ MOO | *www.moo.com*
* ★ Printing.com | *www.printing.com*

★ Vistaprint | *www.vistaprint.co.uk*

★ Staples copy & print centres | *www.staples.co.uk/copy-print*

TIP: A memorable exchange

Richard Moross, founder of MOO.com, says:

> "The point of having a business card is to make a connection, create a relationship and leave something with the recipient that reminds them of you. Have cards that tell a story. Use that card as a sales tool, for sure, but also show appreciation by having cards relating to your customer."

Richard Moross achieves this by having images on his cards showing places he's visited and meals he's eaten. With 70% of MOO's business being outside the UK, Richard travels a lot and the cards act as the ice-breaker in meetings as he tells the story behind the pictures.

In person

You are about to attend your first networking event or trade show and want to create a good first impression. With an attractive business card in hand, directing prospective customers to a good-looking online presence, all you have to do is follow the rules of effective networking!

The art of networking

★ Wear your name tag (if you have one) on your right side. It's easy to catch sight of when you are shaking hands.

★ Deliver a nice firm handshake and make eye contact.

- ★ Say your name clearly and, in under ten seconds, tell the other person who you are and what you do.

- ★ Listen carefully. Ask the other person plenty of questions about their line of business, their family, their hobbies, without being too intrusive or personal.

- ★ Be positive and energetic.

- ★ Swap business cards.

- ★ Send a 'thank you' email after the event, confirming any actions you and they have promised.

- ★ Keep in regular, and meaningful, contact.

Chapter Nine

Happy customers and a balanced business – a recipe for success

I n this section we look at how to keep customers coming back and keeping the business in balance as a stepping stone to growth.

ATTRACT CUSTOMERS BACK

You are making sales via your site and developing a strong community of fans and followers. Give visitors and customers a reason to return by following these steps.

Fresh and user-generated content

Encourage visitors and customers back to your site with regular posted content, and if it's an e-commerce site, keep the product range updated. Give your site some TLC each day, as fresh content will attract visitors who want to see what's new and will also appeal to the trawling web spiders who determine search engine results.

Encourage your site visitors to get to know each other through a forum, comment boxes or a plug-in application. Before you know it, a sense of community will develop and visitors will log on each day to find out who's saying what and what's happening with whom.

Exclusive offers

Extend offers to your existing customers, readers or members that will tempt them back. This offer could be conditional on customers referring a friend: that way your customer returns to the site with others in tow. Add to this with a badge of honour; design an icon that visitors can display on their own site to show their affiliation with you.

Guest appearances

Invite special guests to appear on your site via guest blog posts, hosting a webchat or a featured interview.

Keep in touch

Communicate all these good and 'sticky' things to your users through a regular e-newsletter powered by products such as MailChimp (*www.mailchimp.com*) or AWeber Communications (*www.aweber.com*).

KEEP THE BUSINESS IN BALANCE

As the business continues to grow, you will want to maintain momentum and grow at a comfortable pace. Achieve this by following what I call 'the golden triangle', which will keep you and the business in balance. This requires spending roughly a third of your time on three key things:

1. Customer care

Look after your customers by delivering a quality product or service, on time and within budget. And remember … the customer is always right!

I ask clients for feedback so that I can keep a check on what they're thinking and changes they'd like to see. It's good to know some personal details about your customers, too. (Maybe the date of their birthday, their favourite hobby or names of their children.) As you gather these details, make a quick note so that you can send a birthday card on the right date, enquire after GCSE results at the right time, etc. Don't go overboard, but showing that you care certainly won't harm your relationship.

Offer customers good service, regular communication and an innovative line of products and services. It will stand you in good stead.

2. New business

Taking care of customers means taking care of sales. Why? Because it costs less to win business from existing customers than it does to find new ones. And if customers are happy, they'll say good things about you to new and potential customers. This is called word-of-mouth marketing and achieving it is every business owner's dream!

Secure new clients through marketing, encouraging recommendations and direct-sales calls and pitches.

3. Admin

Not as enjoyable as the first two, but it still has to be done. Keep the books in order by raising invoices in good time, being on top of cash flow and filing tax returns and company documents on time and in order. In short, keep the finances in check and the books up-to-date.

Cash is king

Keep an eye on the accounts so you can see how much money is in the bank, how much is owed and whether this covers your outgoings.

Invoices

Be on time with invoicing and keep a record of amounts outstanding. I have a simple spreadsheet with five columns labelled 'client', 'invoice amount', 'invoice number', 'date submitted' and 'date paid'. *See page 95 for a template invoice reporting sheet.*

Your invoices should be a simple document with basic but thorough details. The less cause for question on the invoice, the faster it will be paid!

Settle invoices as promptly as you can but make use of the credit extended to you. Your suppliers will be grateful and should repay you with good service.

You can balance the budget with a piece of accounting software. Priced at between £50 and £100 for 'starter' versions, these packages offer sales and expense tracking, invoice templates, bank reconciliations and basic bookkeeping. *See pages 244–5 for details of options.*

Receipts

Keep business-related receipts in a place where they're easy to find. I have a big wicker box that doubles as a collecting place for receipts. It's helpful that they're all in one place when it's time to do the VAT return.

Right on time

Without the old framework of office life, you'll want to keep a grasp on time: planning it, tracking it, and definitely making the most of it. Do so with these on and offline technology solutions.

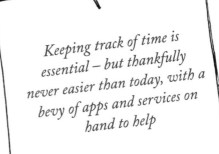

Keeping track of time is essential – but thankfully never easier than today, with a bevy of apps and services on hand to help

FreshBooks

An application that tracks the time you spend on projects and turns this into professional looking invoices. Particularly useful for businesses providing professional and business services.

★ *www.freshbooks.com*

Remember the milk

Take your task list with you and add to it from anywhere with this nifty web-based task manager that synchs with Google Calendar, Twitter, BlackBerry, iPhone, instant messenger, email and text messages. The basic package is free.

★ *www.rememberthemilk.com*

Other time tracking software

* Cashboard | *www.getcashboard.com*

* Four Four Time | *www.fourfourtime.co.uk*

* TraxTime | *www.spudcity.com/traxtime*

If, like me, you're still a pen-and-paper person invest in a diary, filofax or wall calendar from stores such as Staples, Rymans or Paperchase.

TIP: Bug business

Save time and keep customers happy by having bookings taken by a resource such as BookingBug (*www.bookingbug.com*), an online service that allows you to take and manage bookings anytime and from anywhere.

Chapter Ten

Grow the business without outgrowing home

Your business is getting known and making money and you're looking at options on how to scale and grow. Achieve this through:

* Product-ising

* Going global

* Outsourcing

PRODUCT-ISING

If you're making handmade goods or selling knowledge, you'll have soon realised there's only one of you and you can sell only as much as you can make! As scientists haven't yet worked out how to make more of you, in order to grow the business take the knowledge/skill/talent you have and put it in a box!

Kits

Let's take the example of someone making unique dresses for girls; continue to make your signature style dress that is made by your own hands and at a price to reflect your time and dedication, but consider adding to the range with a dress kit that can be bought complete with material and clear instructions so parents can enjoy the experience of buying the kit and making their own dress whilst you enjoy selling more products (admittedly at a lower price) that have not taken as long to produce. At the end of the instructions you could also include details of where people can upload pictures of their creations to your blog or website, creating a sense of community and expanding the reach of your brand.

This is what Carol Powell has done (profiled on page 23) with her Re-jigged Tanktop in a Tin and it's what Kitchen Table Talent Award winner, Katherine Prentice, is now considering.

> "I have a full-time job and am building the business in my spare time so I have to be sure the business can grow in the time I have available to offer. It's for that reason I've decided to continue making my products – handbooks, notebooks and purses – that will come with my signature but I'm also developing kits as I can make these in higher volumes and at a fraction of the cost. The good thing is the kits will work to promote my brand, generate revenue and ensure my products reach a wider number of people. For me, it feels the right way to go and grow!"

★ *www.katherineprenticedesigns.co.uk*

Courses

Maybe you're selling works of art or making jam and want to 'productise' – in which case, how about launching and teaching a class as an ideal way to expand? You get to meet customers and have an opportunity to talk to the press/promote classes in the media and have your name and brand appear in front of more people. You can even sell your produce at the classes!

When it comes to looking for space for such a class, consider your own home or approach the owner of the local coffee shop to ask if he would be happy for you to use the space at times when they are usually quiet; that way you're likely to get space for free in return for introducing footfall. Other places to consider could be your library, community centre/church hall or even a local business. Arianna Cadwallader chose the local pub to run her Saturday Sewing Session!

Talent into turnover

NAME: ARIANNA CADWALLADER
TALENT: SEWING
BUSINESS: SATURDAY SEWING SESSION

At the age of 29, Arianna Cadwallader is a maker and milliner specialising in bespoke wedding dresses and head pieces. "Although my head is in the 21st century," she says, "my heart is firmly in the 1940s. I have a passion for skills that are not used so much anymore; quilting, knitting, sewing, crochet and dressmaking."

With this love of craft and all things handmade, Arianna wanted to create a workshop that would enable and encourage modern women (and men!) to learn these creative arts. To achieve this, she launched Saturday Sewing Session, after seeing a number of similar successful ventures and spotting a gap in the market in her area.

She first came to the attention of Enterprise Nation after submitting an entry to the Ideas 101 competition run in conjunction with PayPal. Her entry shows just how inventive you can be when operating on a budget.

> "I have managed to secure a great room for free above the Chelsea Ram pub (on a quiet day, so it brings them business). I have also secured a partnership with Battersea sewing centre for the hire of machines at half price (I advertise them in my sessions). I am also in the process of getting a deal with a gorgeous cake shop, with free cakes in return for promotion.

"I am in *Time Out* online, I have a Twitter account, Facebook page and blog, and I distribute flyers in places my target audience go. I send out emails to my database and attend start-up business events to network. I have got some upcoming promotion in online and hard-copy magazines and I email relevant companies to see if they are interested in coming onboard."

Arianna gives credit to a network of friends and family in helping achieve her goals: "My boyfriend is an expert in marketing and has brilliant organisational skills. The support from him and my friends and family has been unwavering; they help me prioritise class schedules, materials, ideas for workshops and build up business relationships. They are my constant source of inspiration."

★ *www.saturdaysewingsession.co.uk*

Once you have a space, let people know about the classes. Promote it on your website or blog, include a note in packages sent out, write a release/blog post for the media and local business sites and make the most of local noticeboards, etc. Provide contact details so people can get in touch for more information and to book, and there you have it – you've set up an income earning and brand extending class!

When in the business of providing business services, you can package your knowledge to enable customers to buy your bite-sized advice/tips in box format or hire you for the real thing. The options offered on page 200 for publishing are the best route for you to follow to spread knowledge to a wider audience, i.e. publishing a book, producing a podcast, and charging amounts for people to access this content.

GOING GLOBAL

With exchange rates in our favour and enabling technology to hand, there's never been a better time to look beyond domestic shores for business. By virtue of having a professional window to the world (i.e. website), start-ups and small businesses are going global faster than ever before. In my book, *Go Global: How to take your business to the world*, I show how you can increase trade and broaden horizons in five simple steps. You will also find a free *Go Global* eBook on Enterprise Nation and a downloadable app – all the tools you need to be running an internationally successful business!

OUTSOURCING

Grow profits by focusing on what you do best and outsourcing the rest. It's perfectly possible to achieve this and manage an expanding team from your own small office/home office.

Teamwork saves time

The business is growing, time is your most precious resource and you are in need of help. The quickest and most affordable place to get it is from other companies with whom you can partner to get projects done, as well as from accredited advisors who will offer advice on how the business can continue to grow.

With outsourcing you can free yourself up to dedicate your attention to sales, strategy or whatever the business activity is that you do best. My advice to all businesses is always: focus on what you do best and outsource the rest.

What can be outsourced, and to whom?

Admin

Hire a VA (virtual assistant) to do the admin tasks you don't want or don't have the time to do. Visit VA directories and resources to find your perfect match.

* International Association of Virtual Assistants | *www.iava.org.uk*

* Society of Virtual Assistants | *www.societyofvirtualassistants.co.uk*

* Time Etc | *www.timeetc.co.uk*

* VA Success Group | *www.vasuccessgroup.co.uk*

* Virtual Assistant Chamber of Commerce | *www.virtualassistantnetworking.com*

* Virtual Assistant Coaching & Training Company | *www.vact.co.uk*

PR, marketing and design

Outsource your PR to a specialist who can be pitching and promoting the business whilst you're at work. Find skilled professionals on directory sites such as Enterprise Nation and Business Smiths or contact companies such as PrPro, Press for Attention and Just In Time PR.

* Enterprise Nation | *www.enterprisenation.com*

* Business Smiths | *www.businesssmiths.co.uk*

* PrPro | *www.prpro.co.uk*

* Press for Attention PR | *www.pressforattention.com*

* Just In Time PR | *www.justintimepr.com*

Sales

Hire a sales expert to make calls, set up appointments and attend trade shows. Find these professionals on Enterprise Nation (*www.enterprisenation.com*), contact telemarketing companies that offer outbound sales calls as a service, or look at sales specialists such as Inside and professionals like Jackie Wade.

* Great Guns | *www.greatgunsmarketing.co.uk*

* Inside | *www.theinsideteam.co.uk*

* Winning Sales | *www.winningsales.co.uk*

Customer service

Looking after your customers is vital, but even that can be outsourced to great effect. Get Satisfaction's tagline is "people-powered customer service" – it provides a web-hosted platform, much like a forum, where customers can ask questions, suggest improvements, report a problem or give praise. It can save you time and money by making customer service an open process that leverages the wisdom of crowds. Questions are answered by other users, rather than you as the site host. You don't want to outsource this completely as it's good to show personal contact with customers, but this is a useful tool that could improve your business as customers offer their feedback.

* *www.getsatisfaction.com*

IT

Spending too many hours trying to fix a single IT problem? Outsource the hassle and save your time, money and blood pressure. Find IT professionals on Enterprise Nation or contact IT support teams connected to the large retailers.

* Geeks-on-Wheels | *www.geeks-on-wheels.com*

* The TechGuys | *www.thetechguys.com*

* Geek Squad | *www.geeksquad.co.uk*

Accounts

Unless you are in the accountancy business, this is almost a must to be outsourced. Monthly payroll, accounts, VAT returns and corporate tax returns all take time and it's time you can't afford or simply don't have. A cost/benefit analysis is likely to show that it's cheaper to outsource to a qualified accountant. Ask around for recommendations of accountants in your area who deliver a quality service at a competitive cost and are registered with the Institute of Chartered Accountants in England and Wales.

For online accounting and invoicing that makes life easier for you and your accountant, check out:

* FreeAgent | *www.freeagentcentral.com*

* KashFlow | *www.kashflow.co.uk*

* Liquid Accounts | *www.liquidaccounts.net*

* QuickBooks | *www.quickbooks.co.uk*

* Sage One | *www.sageone.com/accounts*

And keep track of invoices with the template provided on page 95.

STEPS TO SUCCESSFUL OUTSOURCING

Do the groundwork

Spend some time working on the task yourself so that you've built some foundations before handing it over to a third party. For example, if you outsource sales then have a ready-made contacts list and some open doors that the specialist can build on, rather than starting from scratch. This will make it more cost-effective for you and means they hit the ground running; it's not a contract from a cold start, you have already done the groundwork.

Be clear on the brief

Having spent some time doing the task yourself, you will have a clear idea of the brief. Back to the example of outsourcing sales, if you've spent 6 to 12 months sourcing leads and making contacts, you'll have a much clearer idea of the type of prospecting the specialist should do. The clearer the brief, the better the results.

Take your time

And take references. Spend time evaluating the specialists in the market and, if you can, talk to their existing clients. Do they have the industry experience you're after? Will they represent your brand in a professional manner? Have they shown commitment to other clients? When an outsourced arrangement works well, the partner becomes part of your team so choose them as carefully as you would choose an employee.

Let go!

Outsourcing a key function means having to let go a little. Someone else becomes accountable for these results. Embrace this rather than resist it. As the business owner you remain in ultimate control but the expert will need their own space in which to flourish. Outsourcing can save you time and help make you money. Finding the right partner, on the right terms, will make you feel like a new and liberated person.

Form teams

Once you've chosen your outsourced partner(s), it's important to keep in regular contact and work together as a team. There are a number of online project management and collaboration tools to help you stay on top of projects and in control of the company.

Basecamp

The project management tool we rely on at Enterprise Nation. This is a top-class product that allows you to create projects, invite people to view them, upload files and make comments. It's effective online project management that can be accessed from anywhere.

★ *www.basecamphq.com*

Google Docs

Share documents via Google with Google Docs. You can edit on the move, choose who accesses documents and share changes in real-time.

★ *docs.google.com*

Huddle

Offers simple and secure online workspaces. Huddle is hosted, so there's no software to download and it's free to get started.

★ *www.huddle.com*

Solutions to enable group-talk

GoToMeeting

Work with anyone, anywhere with this easy to use online meeting tool.

★ *www.gotomeeting.com*

Ketchup

Share and record meeting notes.

★ *www.useketchup.com*

Pow Wow Now

Free conference calling at 'open access' level. Priced packages available.

★ *www.powwownow.co.uk*

Skype

Free and easy-to-use conference calls for Skype users.

★ *www.skype.com/allfeatures/conferencecall*

TIP: Help from an entern

If you have a project requiring specialist skill or attention consider hiring an entern. Enterns are enthusiastic students and graduates, passionate about entrepreneurship and looking for work experience in young start up companies.

★ *www.enternships.com*

Form partnerships

If relationships with other companies and self-employed professionals develop you may decide to form a partnership. Consider writing a partnership agreement as your 'pre-nup' in business. At the outset of a relationship, all is good and you're excited about the potential, but it's best to be safe; have a few things written and agreed so all parties are clear on expectations.

The following should not be taken as concrete legal advice, more of a guideline on how to draw up an agreement. An agreement need only be a single page and cover the basics:

Scope of agreement

What is your partnership working to achieve? For example, "This agreement is made between Company A and Company B. The agreement is related to the generation of online advertising revenues/hosting of an event/development of a new product."

Respective responsibilities

Set out the expectations on who does what. For example, Company A will be responsible for promotion and business development and Company B will take on technical development and client care. Also include a note of how you'll keep each other briefed, maybe through the use of an online project management tool such as Basecamp.

Finances

What will be the split in revenue, and is this before or after costs? And who owns the intellectual property of the product/service/activity? Consider including a clause that states the agreement will be reviewed in six months so that both parties can check on progress and have the right to cease the agreement if it hasn't gone as planned.

Be fair

Agreements where both parties feel they're receiving their fair share are likely to be longer-lasting than those when one party feels embittered. Talk about this before writing and concluding the agreement. Make sure there's no resentment or sense of being exploited on either side.

Sign it!

After making the effort to produce an agreement, be sure to both sign it! And then store it so you can access it easily if the need arises.

When writing the clauses in your agreement, think about all the things that could go wrong and safeguard against them. It's a practical exercise and won't harm your newly formed business relationship but will get it off on a firm footing. If you're looking for a template agreement, check out the following sites:

* Clickdocs | *www.clickdocs.co.uk*

* Off to see my lawyer | *www.offtoseemylawyer.com*

Talent into turnover

NAME: SARAH THOMAS
TALENT: PHOTOGRAPHY
BUSINESS: SARAH J. THOMAS PHOTOGRAPHY

Sarah Thomas has been interested in art and photography for as long as she can remember.

"When I received my first camera at the age of 8, I threw myself into it, seeing it as an extension of what I was already doing with pencils and paint. I pursued my skill in art to degree level where I achieved a degree in graphic design with a specialism in photography in 1993."

When asked how long it took for the talent to become a business, Sarah replies "only about 35 years!" After leaving university, Sarah opted to take a 'real' job rather than pursue a career as an artist. Through various part-time jobs, she realised she had another skill.

> "I could sell and people would pay me a nice salary to sell. That was the start of my 20-year journey through fashion retail, recruitment and personnel management. Throughout this time my passion for photography remained and as I started a family I began to *really* value the power of images, not just as an art form but also as a way of documenting my precious little people as they grew."

When pregnant with her youngest son (now 4 years old) Sarah was offered redundancy from her job, which she decided to take. With strong support from her family, Sarah embarked on starting her own business, feeling she was finally ready, having developed a wealth of experience in sales, management, art training and, Sarah says, the invaluable skills every parent gains, "patience, determination and effective negotiation!"

Initially the aim was to earn enough to pay for a nice family holiday whilst having the luxury of being a stay-at-home mum, but this business owner underestimated how successful the business would become in a relatively short period of time and is proud to say the business is now a fully fledged career making a healthy profit year on year.

Sarah specialises in family photography; a specialism that came about after spotting a gap in the market.

> "As a parent myself, I remember dragging my children kicking and screaming to the local photographers. I watched them pull the most ridiculous false smiles whilst sitting on a white backdrop and I was always disappointed with the results. I wanted to produce something different, something real, showing my children as they really were. It wasn't until I started producing images myself and showing friends and family that I understood that it wasn't just me – most people wanted something more unique.

"I am good with kids. Actually, I am a people person full stop so there was never any doubt in my mind that I would focus on families. I think it is important to be able to empathise with your customer. Children are unpredictable little things and I seem to be able to have the knack of getting the best from them and dealing with the worst. Parents comment on my patience and I think that speaks volumes about why I chose to specialise and put all my efforts into this area of photography."

Sarah promotes the business through forging relationships and partnerships with likeminded business and organisations targeting the same market, and word of mouth recommendations are the best source of new business. Sarah can also claim a strong track record in repeat business based on the quality of the service she offers.

"What I do is very personal. I am being invited into people's homes, offered the opportunity to play, interact and ultimately capture the essence of their children – service and trust is key. As a result of this focus I have found that 65% of my new business is gained via word of mouth and another 45% of my customers return for a second session within 18 months of our initial meeting."

Identity is also a key element in company promotion and as a trained graphic designer Sarah understands the importance of brand and aims to portray a consistent image for her business. The company has a stylish and professional-looking website (*www.sarahjthomas.com*) and Facebook has also been a critical tool, enabling Sarah to interact with customers, potential clients and fellow photographers for free.

"Alongside my blog (*www.sarahjthomas.blogspot.com*), I aim to use these avenues as a way of showing a bit of the real me – a little more of my personality. I have heard it said that your website should be your handshake and your blog should be a big fat hug. I think it's important for people to understand a little more about what makes you tick, after all – people buy from people."

Sarah is looking forward to an exciting upcoming 12 months and with the company growing at its current pace, is expecting the business to become her full-time career during 2012. She certainly sees the benefits of being able to mould the business around the family and be in control of the pace of company growth.

> "My initial business plan was to build up the business slowly, working part-time before my youngest started full-time school. I always wanted to develop a strong business model during this period, making all the inevitable mistakes early on so I could move forward with my full-time enterprise."

This business owner is in control of a blossoming company and is enjoying the thrills, challenges and opportunities that are all part of the ride.

Top tip

> "Have belief in the value of what you do. If you don't have belief then it's likely that your customer will feel the same. You need to develop confidence in what you do and understand the value of what you produce and the perceived value that your customer places on your work. Never undersell yourself or your talent.

> "You must wear so many hats to make a success of your talent. You have to be an accountant, procurement expert, negotiator, marketing guru, sales person, etc. etc. If you don't possess these skills then don't be scared to outsource them to someone who can – you can't do everything well. Learn to let go. That's very hard and I am not convinced I am quite there yet myself!"

★ *www.sarahjthomas.com* | @sarah_j_thomas

SEEK HELP AND SUPPORT

As a tweet to me once said "asking for help does not make you weak, but it could make you a success". Ask questions at every opportunity; of your peers, of mentors and accredited business advisors. Here's where to find them.

Peers

Who better to turn to than those who are also going through the experience of starting and growing a business? Visit the sites below and join their active forums and communities of business owners who will be more than happy to help.

* BusinessZone | *www.businesszone.co.uk*
* Start Up Donut | *www.startupdonut.co.uk*
* *Business Matters* magazine | *www.bmmagazine.co.uk*
* In a fishbowl | *www.inafishbowl.com*
* Enterprise Nation | *www.enterprisenation.com*

Mentors

The coalition government has announced a national mentoring programme and the recruitment of no less than 40,000 mentors who will be on hand to help young and start-up businesses.

* Mentorsme | *www.mentorsme.co.uk*

TIP: Support from The Supper Club

One of the most popular offers made on the launch of national campaign StartUp Britain was the offer of 1,000 mentoring hours from members of The Supper Club. Founder Duncan Cheatle says:

"Our members are successful business owners who are willing and able to help the next generation of entrepreneurs. They are doing this through offering their time and mentoring start-ups via calls or meeting face-to-face. The purpose is for the start up to describe their business and outline aims, and for the more experienced business owner to offer feedback and direction. It's proving to be incredibly popular and is an effective way to transfer skills from one business owner to another."

★ *www.preludegroup.co.uk/what-we-do/start-up-britain*

Thoughts on a mentor

Over the ten-years-plus of running my own business, I have developed a view on mentors. It may not be a view with which you agree, as each business owner is different. But this is what has worked for me.

Don't restrict yourself to one mentor! I have learnt from many people as my businesses have passed through different stages of development. I would approach the person I felt best placed to have the answer, take on board their views, consider my options, and then act.

The ideal mentor is someone who possesses four things:

1. experience of your industry/sector
2. the ability to listen

3. the technical skills to advise

4. a willingness to make introductions to useful contacts.

If you can find these in one person, you are a fortunate person. One of the finest things a mentor can do is allow you to talk. By doing so, you will often find you work out the answer. You sometimes just need a sounding board to answer your own question.

Accredited advisors

When starting and growing your business, consider approaching your local enterprise agency for support. The National Enterprise Network acts as an umbrella organisation for all agencies so you can find your local contact at *www.nfea.com*. Local business advisors can help with everything from business planning to applying for funds and financial forecasting.

★ *www.nationalenterprisenetwork.co.uk*

StartUp Britain

In March 2011, a national campaign was launched to encourage more people to start a business and support existing businesses to grow. The campaign is run by a team of eight business owners and entrepreneurs, with support from the government and a number of corporate sponsors.

The face of the campaign is a website which offers links to useful resources and content, as well as valuable offers from large corporates and leading brands. Visit the site to be inspired and to celebrate the start-ups of Britain.

★ *www.startupbritain.org*

Enterprise Nation

Turn to Enterprise Nation as your central resource and friend in business. Every month we:

* profile small business success stories

* release eBooks on topics that matter most

* produce videos with bite-size business advice

* host webchats with experts and special guests

* develop new tools to help you increase sales and reduce costs

* connect you to peers via forums and our friendly marketplace.

Enterprise Nation is the place where you can access advice and support, raise profile and make sales.

* *www.enterprisenation.com* | @e_nation

Group together for discounts

The concept of group buying online is still in its infancy says Alex Harrington-Griffin of *BusinessCrayon.com*, but websites like Groupon have shown what's possible.

Alex's site is one of an increasing number of websites where small businesses can come together to buy in bulk and benefit from volume discounts. Deals are on offer and when that deal hits the target number of small businesses willing to buy, then the supplier is committed to providing the product/service at the price proposed.

Check out the sites below to access and activate deals

* Business Crayon | *www.businesscrayon.com*

* Huddlebuy | *www.huddlebuy.co.uk*

* SME Discounts | *www.smediscounts.com*

Foodie Friends

There's a new kind of support for food-based businesses in the form of the Food Funnel developed by digital agency JumpTo! who are connecting young businesses with large retail channels, media contacts and food trend-setters and spotters. For anyone starting and growing a food based business, this is a tasty option!

* *www.jumpto.co.uk*